Clergy
Personal
Finance

Clergy Personal Finance

WAYNE C. BARRETT

Abingdon Press
Nashville

CLERGY PERSONAL FINANCE

Copyright © 1990 by Abingdon Press

This book is printed on acid-free paper.

Library of Congress Cataloging-in-Publication Data

Barrett, Wayne C., 1947-
    Clergy personal finance / Wayne C. Barrett.
    p. cm.
    ISBN 0-687-08669-8 (alk. paper)
    1. Clergy—Finance. Personal. I. Title.
    BV4397.B33 1990
    332.024'2—dc20   90-35096
                                                      CIP

Cartoons on pp. 44 and 78 are reprinted by permission of Tribune Media Services.

Cartoon on p. 111 is from *Instant Cartoons for Church Newsletters No. 1* by George Knight. Copyright © 1982 by Baker Book House. Used by permission.

Cartoons on pp. 61 and 114 are from *Instant Cartoons for Church Newsletters No. 2* by George Knight. Copyright © 1984 by Baker Book House. Used by permission.

MANUFACTURED IN THE UNITED STATES OF AMERICA

Acknowledgments

This work is the collaboration of this writer and literally hundreds of clergy, whose questions and comments at seminars across the country have helped to increase and sharpen my awareness of the critical issues confronting the clergy today.

I am particularly appreciative of the outstanding work of Peggy Patterson, my administrative assistant, who created and shaped the manuscript for this volume. I acknowledge the assistance of my partner and colleague, Charles Fry, who contributed major portions of chapters 6 and 10.

I could not have completed this project without my yeoman editor, Paul Franklyn, who encouraged me and guided this work to its completion.

Finally, I am grateful for the support and encouragement of my family—Linda, Chris, Joel, and Andrea—who tolerated my hours at the word processor when we should have been vacationing.

Contents

Foreword

No, it's not your low income that's the problem. Nor is it taxes, the parsonage, or any of the other excuses that frequently appear to be the culprit that's really the trouble. The reason so many clergy find their finances out of control is the lack of a workable financial plan. It is the plan, after all, that enables us to get where we want to be no matter where we're starting from.

In financial planning sessions with hundreds of clergypersons we often hear the assumption that increased levels of income would solve the problem. Yet, this is nearly always a naive expectation. Professional credit counselors have established the fact that persons go into bankruptcy at all levels of the income ladder. Low income debtors are confident that an extra $25 a week would take care of their dilemma. At the same time, a family is going broke on an income of six figures—all the while certain that their problem is nothing that an extra $10,000 couldn't cure. Clearly, the solution to the common problem is not merely additional income. I believe the solution is financial planning.

What Is Financial Planning?

The pastor in a church where I was speaking one Sunday surprised me and confused the congregation by making this announcement: "After the service the Reverend Barrett will lead us in a session on family planning!" Whether or not she or the congregation had a need for family planning I do not know, but I am confident that financial planning is a separate discipline. By financial planning I refer to a process of collecting data about our financial lives, monitoring our income and spending patterns, establishing goals and, finally, creating strategies that enable us to reach the goals we've set.

Financial planning for the clergy involves taking an honest look at our values and goals, learning how to utilize resources that are available to us, and making adaptations in our spending and investing that result in connecting where we are with where we wish to be.

Can it work for you? Of course. *Will* it work for you? That is entirely up to you. In this book I will attempt to present financial planning techniques that are proven winners. My goal is to present the material free of jargon and inside language so that you will find immediate help. Sound interesting? Let's get started.

Clergy
Personal
Finance

1

A Theology
of Money

Clergy face the task of financial planning with a certain ambiguity. On the one hand, few clergy enter the profession with much experience (or interest) in the financial sciences. Yet, clergy must pay their bills with real money like everybody else. The very same pastors who would prefer to "take no thought for the morrow" are the ones who discover that retirement is approaching, whether they are ready or not.

To further complicate the matter, the traditions of itineracy and parsonage residency provide financial pitfalls for the clergy that are virtually unique in our society. Whereas the laity build their financial plans around the cornerstone of home ownership, the clergy are seldom afforded this prerogative. The task of financial planning for the clergy is different, but it can be equally rewarding as we become comfortable with money and its role in enabling a wide variety of life-style opportunities.

Let us, therefore, begin our explorations into the world of personal finance from a perspective with which the pastor may feel more familiar: Christian theology.

A Theological Case for Financial Planning

In Matthew 25 Jesus told a story in the form of a parable. There were ten young women who had been invited to a wedding feast. Because people had a more relaxed attitude toward time in those days, the women had gotten together to await the feast. Each of the ten women had brought lamps, but only five had remembered to bring oil, and without oil, a lamp was useless. We can only ponder the feelings of those who, upon hearing the call to come to the wedding feast, found themselves left behind in the dark. I doubt that any of these young women planned to be left behind. Each had probably rationalized that she would not really need the oil, or that one of the others would share, or perhaps that the feast would never take place anyway. Whatever the reasons, the results were all the same: tragedy—an opportunity squandered for lack of preparation and planning.

In my work with clergy I have become aware that this phenomenon is not limited to first-century women. Many are the modern clergypersons—men and women alike—who go through their careers in constant financial jeopardy because they have not prepared themselves. Frequently I meet clergy with the equivalent of an empty lamp—perhaps an I.R.A. (Individual Retirement Account) to which they have contributed nothing since 1983. They have the tools but lack the plans to enable the tools to become most useful.

The wise use and management of financial resources is based upon a solid biblical principle: Christian stewardship. The scriptural image of money cannot be characterized as positive or negative since both examples abound. What is clear, however, is that the use of resources is intended to be prudent and rooted in an awareness of God's ultimate ownership.

Clergy, then, are called to exercise wise stewardship of financial resources. Their goal is not the accumulation of enormous wealth but rather the achievement of family and faith goals. Money is never the end but is the means to a variety of worthy goals.

Perhaps it will be helpful for the clergyperson to remember this means/end distinction as we continue this examination of a Christian view toward wealth. It is not wealth that we seek, but rather the liberation that financial health brings. Clergy often fail to remember that the priesthood has evolved in substantial ways since the apostle Paul. Although we are called into a similar faith commitment, the life of modern Protestant clergy is no longer presumed to be one of celibate singleness.

Whereas ancient clerics may have been free to adopt lives of asceticism and poverty, it is not likely that today's minister has the right to presume his or her spouse and family want lives of such impoverishment.

" HE WAS ONE OF OUR MOST PROMISING MINISTERS! THEN HIS VOW OF POVERTY 'BECAME AN OBSESSION' "

It is not avarice or materialism that motivates the modern clergyperson to practice financial planning; rather, it is a healthy appreciation for the salutary effect upon one's ministry that financial health produces. I think Robert Kemper is correct when he observes that an almost inevitable outcome of low clergy income and its attendant financial tensions is that clergy become materialistic![1] It could hardly be otherwise. When money is tight in the parsonage and the monthly ritual of juggling dental bills, car payments, and bank card installments becomes a major concern, the clergy find life

---

1. Robert G. Kemper, *The New Shape of Ministry* (Nashville: Abingdon, 1979).

dominated by dollar signs. The very same clerics who wish to be people oriented become money dominated when "making ends meet" consumes their passions.

When my business partner and I formed our corporation a number of years ago, we did so with the expressed goal of helping clergy more effectively manage their financial resources in order to become more effective ministers of Jesus Christ. Over the years we have discovered that energies that might have enabled some persons to find success and satisfaction in parish ministry have, instead, often been squandered in a variety of financial schemes. These ill-conceived schemes usually become attractive only after finances seem out of control. My hope is that you might gain control of your money early in your career in ministry and become freed up for a more effective life of service.

Along the way you learn to feel more comfortable with money as you experience its potential to enrich as well as enslave. Success in managing your personal finances almost inevitably results in increased skill in administering the finances of your congregation. In fact, a Christian layman friend of mine once remarked that the best way to solve the financial problems of most of our congregations would be to assist the pastors to gain control of their personal finances. I think he is right.

I suspect that the basis for this change in behavior may be attitudinal. When money is seen as the enemy, we either retreat from its influence into a shadowy kind of asceticism, or we attack it blindly by subscribing to the first get-rich-quick scheme that presents itself. Either way we miss the point: money is not the enemy. It is merely a tool that, when skillfully wielded, enables, or, when clumsily managed, ensnares. Recognizing how wealth really works may enable you to change your attitude about your money and your ministry.

Finally, learning to handle money as an expression of stewardship can give meaning and perspective to a task that otherwise may appear foreboding and sterile. We learn to manage our money because it's a faithful way to manage our lives.

2

Getting Started

I used to have a poster in my office to remind me of the greatest obstacle to success in virtually any endeavor. The poster was a photograph of a huge ugly frog, and below that frog's picture were these words: "Thought for the day: If you plan to swallow a frog, it is best not to look at it too long."

Yes, it's true. The hardest part of the task of financial planning is getting started. The longer we ponder the task, the more formidable and intimidating it becomes, and, regrettably, the less likely we are ever to begin the journey toward economic health. You've come this far; you've acquired this book and begun the journey—don't quit now.

The First Step

The initial step in our journey toward economic health is to take stock of where we are now. This will require an honest look at our habits, our values, and our goals. We will discover our financial strengths and will boldly address our weaknesses. Let's find out how much we know about ourselves and our money.

For the next two minutes take a financial inventory of all you possess—the assets and the liabilities. Financial planners call this inventory a statement of net worth. Accountants call it a balance sheet. Let's just think of it as the first step.

Create two columns on a page. In the left column, under the

heading "Assets," list everything that you own. Don't worry about the order yet, just begin to write down everything you can think of that you own. Be sure to include assets such as bank accounts (including checking account balances), C.D.s (Certificates of Deposit), mutual funds and other securities, cash values of life insurance policies, current value of your pension plans (including your I.R.A.s), real estate, and personal property such as cars and furnishings. Remember to value personal property at today's fair market value, not necessarily what you paid for it.

In the right column, under the heading "Liabilities," list any debts that you currently owe. These might include auto loans, credit card balances, mortgages (if you own real estate), and any personal debts such as educational debts.

Total all of your assets and subtract the liabilities to determine your "net worth." This figure may come as quite a shock to you the first time. The number may be substantially less than you had imagined, or it may be comfortably above what you had feared. Don't worry. There is no number that is right or wrong. This is merely where you are beginning the journey. If the net worth total seems low, this probably indicates only that you are relatively young (or are getting a late start)—but don't despair. You can get there from here.

Although this net worth statement is primarily a step in getting started, it serves another important purpose. Updating the statement each year offers a basis for comparison and allows us to evaluate progress. Choose a date each year when you will prepare a new balance sheet. Pick a birthday, anniversary, or some other date when you will update last year's figures. Finding out that you are making progress toward an important goal can be a powerful incentive. When I discover that my plan is working for me, it's like saying "Sic 'em!" to a dog. It makes me all the more determined. On the other hand, if you discover that another year has come and gone with little to show for it, the balance sheet may be the objective proof you need to see the error of your ways.

Here's an example of a balance sheet that may help you get started. Notice that we have divided all of the assets into three categories: cash, investments, and use assets. The purpose of this division will become clear in later chapters. For now, let's define what we mean by each term. Cash is anything that is in the form of cash or can be readily converted into cash with no loss of principle. Examples of cash are bank savings accounts, checking accounts, money market funds, and other funds that are readily liquid. Use assets are items which, while having value, are already committed for some use other than your financial planning goals. Examples of use assets include furniture and appliances, automobiles, and collectibles you are unwilling to sell—heirlooms, for instance. Investments are virtually anything that is not cash or a use asset.

BALANCE SHEET

John and Jane Smith

December 31, 1989

ASSETS		LIABILITIES	
Cash and Cash Equivalents		Auto loan 1	$4,600
Savings account	$1,840	Auto loan 2	1,800
Checking account	1,100	Visa	1,200
		Student loan	2,800
Invested Assets			
Savings bonds	1,200	Total Liabilities	$10,400
C.D.	3,000		
Pension fund	13,000	Net Worth	$46,940
I.R.A.	3,100		
Insurance (cash			
value)	2,100		
Use Assets			
Auto 1	7,500		
Auto 2	3,800		
Boat	1,700		
Furnishings	18,000		
Stamp collection	1,800		
		Total Liabilities and	
Total Assets	$57,340	Net Worth	$57,340

(*Note:* The total liabilities and net worth must always be exactly the same as the total assets. If you do not balance, go back and discover what you have left out. Just remember the basic net worth formula: Assets - Liabilities = Net worth)

BALANCE SHEET

Date _____

ASSETS

Cash on Hand _____
Checking Accts. _____
Savings Accts. _____
Credit Union _____
Other _____
    Total Cash _____

Life Insurance
  Cash Values (total) _____

Company Retirement
  Plan (vested amt.) _____

Securities (market value):
  Stocks _____
  Bonds _____
  Mutual Funds _____
    Total _____

LIABILITIES

Mortgage Balance (home) _____
Other Mortgages _____
Auto Loans _____
Personal Loans _____
Installment Loans (list): _____
_____
_____
_____
    Total _____

Charge Accounts (list): _____
_____
_____
_____
    Total _____

Real Estate (market value):

Home _____

Other _____

Total _____

Automobiles
(market value) _____

Home Furnishings
(market value) _____

Other Personal Property
(market value) _____

Other Assets (itemize): _____

_____

_____

Total _____

TOTAL ASSETS $ _____

Other Outstanding Bills:

Utilities _____

Taxes _____

Misc. _____

Total _____

TOTAL LIABILITIES $ _____

Total Assets $ _____
(minus)

Total Liabilities $ _____
(equals)

NET WORTH $ _____

What do we do now? Check the balance sheet carefully. Is there anything there that is a surprise? What is the distribution of assets? Perhaps you discover that a major portion of your assets is use assets and that most of your invested funds are in the form of pension accounts. This would suggest that adjustments may need to be made in your spending, saving, and investing patterns. Don't feel bad yet—remember, you've made a lot of progress by getting to this point. It is surprising, but nevertheless true, that most people haven't the foggiest idea what their net worth is, much less how it is distributed.

In a culture that reveres materialism, it is amazing that so many persons know so little about their finances. Most people can't even tell you their annual income levels with much accuracy. This is demonstrated through an unusual survey finding. Every ten years the Bureau of the Census takes a poll, and along with a number of other things, asks respondents what the approximate level of family income is. A similar survey is taken annually by the Internal Revenue Service. The questions, although much the same, are asked in completely different circumstances. In the Census, the respondent knows that there is no penalty for guessing high, whereas in the IRS situation (a tax return), the respondent knows that every dollar declared is a dollar upon which taxes must be paid. In these dissimilar circumstances it would be natural to expect the Census-taker to receive higher responses; yet just the opposite occurs. Taxpayers consistently report higher incomes to the IRS than to the Census. Why? Probably because of the slightly different manner in which the question is asked. Whereas the Census asked for a number "off the top of one's head," the tax return requires that the respondent compute the number on paper first. Perhaps this extra step is what results in higher numbers when additional income sources such as overtime pay, interest income, and bonuses are included.

The point of this exercise is to get in touch with your personal finances—good or bad. Learn what you already have before expending any effort to accumulate more.

3

Getting Control of
Your Money

One of the inevitabilities about money is that it never stands still. Money is always moving—toward us or away from us. As one pundit put it, "That money talks I can't deny; it spoke to me and said 'Good-bye.' " One of the critical exercises in creating your financial plan is to discover where your money is going *now*.

Use the Income and Expense Record below to record cash flow for a period of two months. This is the only way you will be able to get a handle on what your money is up to. Creating this record for only one month will seldom be sufficient because few months are truly representative of your on-going spending habits. Something unusual always seems to come up; but, before you discount the unexpected, check a second month and you will see that every month has an unexpected expense. You can't discount the occasional repair or medical expense, because history shows there will always be such costs in any given month.

Although the challenge to keep an expense record for two complete months may seem overwhelming, start with one day. Be utterly ruthless in recording every expense. Note each cup of coffee you buy, each parking meter you feed, and all other out-of-pocket costs. During this period you may wish to cut back on your use of cash. Write a check or use a bank card for gasoline and other routine purchases. This will provide a record—a paper trail—of where the money is really going.

INCOME AND EXPENSE RECORD

	MONTH		MONTH	
	SPENDING PLAN	ACTUAL	SPENDING PLAN	ACTUAL
Income				
Net pay				
Other income				
Total cash available during period				
Fixed Expenses				
Mortgage or rent				
Utilities				
Church and charity				
Life insurance				
Health insurance				
Auto insurance				
Income tax (if not withheld)				
Local and property taxes				
Loan or installment payments				
Savings				
Emergency fund				
Other				
Total Fixed Expenses				

Variable Expenses				
Food				
Clothing				
Household expense				
Medical and dental				
Transportation (including auto operating costs)				
Recreation, vacation				
Gifts				
Personal allowances				
Other				
Total Variable Expenses				
Summary				
Total Cash Available				
Total Expenses				
Cash Balance				

At the end of the day, take a moment to check your results. Any surprises? Perhaps the amount of expenditures from loose cash is higher than you might have predicted, or maybe the daily tab for coffee and donuts is actually $3.50—that's more than $800.00 a year!

Complete this ritual each day until you have a month's worth of experience. Do you notice any spending patterns? For instance, do you spend more when you carry more cash in your pocket? Most people do. Does your spending increase right after payday and cut back near the end of the month when there's nothing left? Your experience here will tell you a lot about your spending habits and will provide valuable clues about where changes must be initiated.

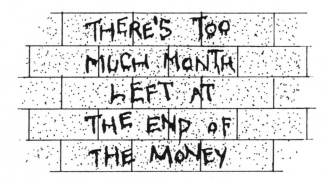

Wailing Wall

Once you have two months experience on paper you should learn some things about yourself. I recall how shocked I was to learn that our family of five—three males and two females—spends an average of $50.00 each month on haircuts. Because I get my hair cut every six weeks at the cheapest barbershop I can find ($7.50 including tip), I had naively assumed that the rest of my clan did likewise. It was a real education to discover that the going rate at the salon my kids frequent is $15.00 plus tip!

How much of your total food bill is spent at restaurants and fast-food counters? Americans spend an average of about 42 cents of every food dollar on these, but there's no law that says you must be average. When your children are young you may find that your restaurant spending is low. Conversely, "empty-nesters" may be seen filling the booths of eateries all across the land. Two-income families tend to eat out more than single-paycheck households. But how much is too much? You may be able to answer this question when you see your monthly total. If you have gross earnings of $2,000 a month and you spend $250 eating out, you may have identified an area for cost reduction.

How about your charitable giving pattern? Did the amount of gifts to church and charity truly represent what your faith means to you? Someone has suggested that the most profound testimony of all is that rendered by our checkbook. What we give to the ministry of our church says a lot about how important it is to us. If the total in your "church and charity" column is not representative of your faith, this too may be an area for some spending changes. More than a few clergy have testified to me that the greatest joy growing out of their successful financial planning was their increased ability to give again.

Now, take a moment to see if you are missing something. It's possible that a random two-month sampling may not include occasional expenditures such as insurance premiums, tax payments, gifts, and other seasonal items. Because you know that these expenses are coming sometime, you will need to include them when you create your spending plan.

How Your Spending Plan Can Save You Money

As you complete your Income and Expense Record, you will begin to notice seasonal expenses. Expenses for birthday and Christmas gifts, vacation, travel, or back-to-school clothing are common costs that most parsonage families experience every year. Whether or not these costs are included in your two-month representative record, you will need to build them into your spending plan along with a variety of other occasional variable expenses. Besides the obvious requirement of having sufficient funds available to make these occasional purchases, setting money aside for anticipated purchases ahead of time can save you money in a variety of ways.

THE HOUSEHOLD BUDGET

Percent of expenditures by category, 1987

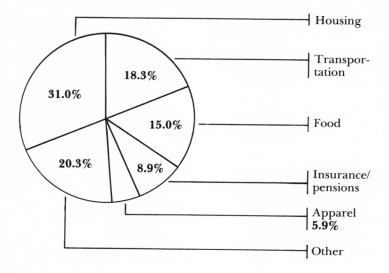

1. You'll avoid interest costs by eliminating the need to borrow or buy on credit. With bank card interest averaging 18%, this strategy alone can be like buying everything on sale.

2. You'll earn interest while the money is on deposit. Even though you'll be investing these short-term funds in super-liquid accounts like money-market or statement savings accounts, any interest is better than no interest.

3. Having money available can enable you to buy when you can get the best price—not when you've got to have the item. Fall may not be the best time to load up on back-to-school items. We always bought winter coats in March when the "50% off" sales started. The coats were for the *following* winter. You will find similar bargains all year long if you've got the money to take advantage of the occasional opportunity.

4. Your plan can be the best defense against impulse buying. One of the worst mistakes people make with money is the ill-conceived impulse purchase. You're in the sporting goods store to buy your son's shoe laces, and suddenly you decide an exercise bike is just what you need to get in shape. A year from now you'll find yourself trying vainly to convince somebody to

pay you $25 for your $200 bike at your garage sale. If such items are not in your plan, you'll need an extraordinary reason to buy them.

My colleagues testify that the total savings from these strategies is like finding an additional fifty cents to spend with every dollar. Sound good? This is why your plan is so important. Get control of your money now.

4

Establishing Financial Goals

O.K., you're ready to establish some financial goals. Where do you begin? Let's start with your values. Unless your goals reflect what you really believe to be important, it is unlikely that you will stick to any plan. *Why* you do anything will, to a large degree, determine *how* you do it.

The legendary Paul "Bear" Bryant was known as a fierce disciplinarian who instilled more than a little fear in his football players. A story about Bryant concerns a particular game when it appeared that Bryant's team had clinched the victory. With the team leading by a field goal, Bryant's quarterback had only to run out the clock to achieve the win. The quarterback, however, could not resist the temptation to attempt one more touchdown pass. The ill-fated pass was intercepted. Not only was it intercepted, but it was intercepted by a defensive back who was the conference 100-yard-dash champion. It appeared that no one would be able to catch the defensive back; yet almost miraculously the quarterback came from out of nowhere to tackle the interceptor and preserve the victory as time expired. After the game, reporters were anxious for Bryant's view. "How," they inquired, "could your quarterback—not known for his footspeed—catch the speed-ster who had intercepted the pass?" Bryant replied, "It's simple. The defensive back was only runnin' for a touchdown. My man was runnin' for his life!"

Why are you running? What values undergird your goals?

In the following goal-setting exercise it is important to include your spouse and, if possible, your children. Money management experts recommend including the children for two significant reasons: (1) Whatever your goals, the children will be affected by them, and (2) this is a great opportunity to teach the youngsters about your values and dreams.

Let me repeat that it is absolutely vital that your spouse participate in this goal-setting. I have seldom worked with a couple in financial difficulty who had ever discussed their individual financial goals with each other. With no sharing of individual goals and dreams, is it any wonder that mutual goals never appear?

Start with your Christian faith. How is your faith to find witness in your financial plan? Are you a tither? If not, is this a worthy goal for your family to work toward? Unless you establish up front that your family will be a giving family, there never will be enough money left to make significant gifts to the church or any other cause. So, a primary value you identify may be giving.

Another primary value in many parsonage families is higher education. College for the children is not considered an option in most clergy households today; it's a given. However, with price tags averaging in excess of $6,000 annually for public universities and $11,000 for private schools, the burden on the family budget is far too great unless this expense is a basic part of the plan. If college is a part of your plan, get started on it early. The headstart can bring even the impossible dream within reach. For example, if you wait until your daughter is a senior in high school to establish a college fund, you will need to put away $716.64 each month for the next five years to pay for a private college education. In most parsonages, that $700 is more than the budget will allow. But what if you had begun the college fund nine years earlier when she was in second grade? The monthly contribution would only need to be $225—a bit easier to reach.

Perhaps the greatest concern expressed by parsonage families in seminars we have resourced is the issue of providing retirement housing. This future liability hangs like a cloud over the heads of all parsonage-dwellers and must be built into your set of financial goals. Knowing that your retirement home is assured can remove the sense of vulnerability experienced by many clergy and their spouses.

Now that you've gotten in touch with your value system, let's start to work on financial goals that are reflective of your values. It may be helpful at this point to think of the financial planning process as a journey and the goal as your destination. In fact, you'll probably discover a number of destinations you want to reach in the journey of financial planning. To place these multiple targets in perspective, let's categorize them according to immediacy.

For our purposes there are three general categories of goals: short-term goals, intermediate goals, and long-term goals. Short-term goals are financial challenges to be met within the next twelve to twenty-four months. These might include the purchase of a new car, retirement of credit card balances, or a family vacation. Intermediate goals are challenges expected in the next two to five years. These might include college expenses or down payments for rental property or a vacation home. Long-term goals are expenses more than five years down the road and could include early retirement or a retirement home. (Use the goal setting blanks at the end of this chapter to differentiate between the three levels of immediacy.)

Before you start to write down anything as a joint goal, take a few moments and create a personal goal statement while your spouse does the same thing. Please don't presume that you're already on the same wavelength. My experience with couples in seminars is that they seldom have really worked out this matter of joint financial goals. Compare each other's responses. It's not unusual for couples to discover seemingly incompatible goals. For example, he says "retirement cottage near a fishing stream," while she says "condo near the grandchildren." Unless the grandchildren live near a trout stream, you've got a problem. But it's a lot easier to address the incongruity of your goals now rather than two years before retirement. It may be possible to achieve both goals if you start early enough and work at it.

More likely, however, you will need to find some compromise. As long as sufficient retirement income will be available, you may be able to rent a fishing cottage for several weeks each year and avoid the need to own. Or, perhaps an honest examination will establish that "near the grandchildren" is a moving target (and potentially illusory if they move to opposite coasts).

Work at creating a narrative statement of your goals. Be specific. It's not enough to say "Long-term goal—house." A better statement would be "Purchase by 1999 a two-bedroom retirement home near children and grandchildren." Or set an intermediate goal like this one: "Four years tuition and expenses at our church-related college commencing 1994."

Now remember that these are financial goals we are establishing, so you must convert each narrative description into a dollar equivalent expressed in terms of the targeted time frame. For example, your two-bedroom retirement home might cost $75,000 today, but that is not your goal. You must project the present value (what it costs today) into the future to establish your financial goal. If your retirement date is ten years from now, the $75,000 house can be presumed to cost $125,000 if prices increase at only a 5% rate ($198,000 if cost increases 10% yearly).

FAMILY FINANCIAL GOALS

Date:

Short-range goals: Goal reached (date):

Intermediate goals: Goal reached (date):

Long-range goals: Goal reached (date):

5

Your Spending Plan

Many financial plans fail because they depend on a strategy that doesn't work. Nearly every book on money management you've ever seen refers to this same strategy. The strategy? A budget. Budgets, folks tell me, are much like diets. Everybody has tried it once or twice and, having failed, concluded that they will never try it again.

I say, "Don't bother creating a budget." Instead, let's try a *spending plan*. You may notice that a spending plan looks suspiciously like a budget. The critical difference is perceptual. Whereas the word *budget*, like the word *diet*, sounds like self-denial and pain, spending plan conversely suggests the reality: you plan to spend. Call me crazy, but a spending plan is more fun than a budget anytime.

To create your spending plan we'll need to use the data you've already gathered about your current spending patterns and the financial goals you've developed. Then we'll adjust the spending pattern into a spending plan that will connect where you are now with where you want to be. A good plan will be specific but also sufficiently flexible to prevent your feeling trapped. Perhaps the reason so many budgets fail is this feeling of confinement most budgets produce. Because your goals will be continually revised, so must your spending plan. Achieving a financial goal frees up cash to be committed to new goals. Conversely, failure to attain a stated goal should prompt a careful examination of the spending plan to determine whether the plan was workable in the first place. Sometimes assumptions you've made prove to be unrealistic while other failures develop because you've sabotaged the plan. For example, we frequently find colleagues who have made little progress toward long-term investment goals because they failed to reinvest interest distributions from the Certificate of Deposit or bond that was intended to achieve the long-term goal.

Now let's create your spending plan. Use the form provided. You may wish to photocopy it. Follow these initial steps.

1. Figure your total monthly income. Remember to include occasional sources like funeral and wedding honoraria. Don't forget interest and dividend income unless these investments are already designated for another purpose.

2. List your regular fixed monthly expenses. Christians include church contributions and other giving as fixed expenses, not because they can't be changed, but because they are basic to our values. Be sure to include taxes unless they are withheld and are not included in your income above. Allocate the proper amount for insurance premiums and other periodic expenses, even if they are not due each month. Accountants call these set-asides for anticipated expenses "accrued liabilities." You can call them anything you want as long as you build them into your spending plan.

3. Create an emergency fund. Put aside a regular amount until you build up a reserve equal to three months' "net cash flow." Net cash flow is income minus savings and investments. It represents what you would live on in an emergency.

4. Savings should be a part of every spending plan. How much you save will depend on your goals and how you're trying to reach them. Just as it may be more helpful to refer to this entire exercise as a spending plan rather than a budget, many people find it easier to call this part "deferred spending." That's really what savings is anyway—funds that you don't spend today are deferred to be spent tomorrow. In our chapter on saving strategies we present fifteen ways you may learn to put aside the funds that will enable your spending plan to connect today with tomorrow. Later in this chapter we will show you how to allocate these savings accounts among appropriate savings and investment instruments.

A. Annual Income:

Net Salary $ _____
(annual pay minus deductions)

Other Income $ _____
(interest, dividends, etc.)

TOTAL ANNUAL INCOME $ _____

TOTAL MONTHLY INCOME $ _____

B. Emergency Fund Goal: $ _____

(to be set aside monthly): $ _____

C. Fixed Expenses:

	JAN	FEB	MAR	APR	MAY	JUN	JUL	AUG	SEP	OCT	NOV	DEC	YEARLY TOTAL
Mortgage or rent													
Utilities													
Church and charity													
Life insurance													
Health insurance													
Auto insurance													
Income tax (if not withheld)													
Local and property tax													
Loan or installment payments													
Savings													
Emergency fund													
Other:													

Total for Year $ _____

To be set aside Monthly $ _____

D. Variable Expenses (monthly):

Food $ _____

Clothing   _____

Household expense   _____

Medical and dental   _____

Auto operating exp.   _____

Recreation, Vacation   _____

Gifts $ _____

Personal allowances   _____

Other: _____

Total Variable Expenses $ _____

SUMMARY:

Monthly income $ _____

Fixed expenses $ _____

Variable expenses $ _____

Monthly Excess or Debit $ _____

Just as tithing may seem impossible to those who've never tithed, saving 10% of your income may seem beyond your reach when you begin your first spending plan. Nevertheless, it is possible for persons to save 10% or more of their income—some people do it regularly. If you're just getting started, consider this: If you started saving 10% of your income at age thirty and continued this percentage until retirement, you would be able to send your children to any college in the nation and still have enough at retirement to buy a new home and live on the same income (or more) as you earned before retirement.

But save something every month. Start with a modest amount—say $25. Don't dismiss this as too little to bother with. This is the seed of your future that you're planting. I remember the wise words of a man who helped me understand saving when he said, "Saving is to investing as seed is to agriculture. Unless you have the seed you'll never grow a crop."

5. Now let's go to the variable expense section. Your Income and Expense Record has shown you that much of the "evaporation" of our money occurs among items in this variable category. Food, for example, includes not only the weekly supermarket bill, but also the donut and coffee at Donut Delite every morning, the $4.75 you give your daughter for school lunches each week, and the pizza you picked up after the movie Friday night.

I encourage you to provide some money for every member of the household to have an allowance. These funds are for personal spending and do not have to be spent for any of these fixed or variable categories. Providing children with regular allowances helps them to see how they fit into the family economic picture and to learn valuable lessons about money management.

How did you come out after totaling each section? After subtracting fixed and variable expenses from your monthly income, are there funds left over or are you in the red? If you are spending more than you earn, you are not alone. A recent study disclosed that among families in the twenty-five to thirty-five age group, the typical family spends $397 each month more than they earn! With credit cards and loans,

Americans of all age brackets spend, on average, 107% of their income every year.

If your income doesn't seem to cover expenses, go back and see if there are variable expenses that can be reduced without too much hardship. You'll have to face reality someday, and it might as well be now. Don't be tempted to slash unrealistically. It's not enough to say, "Let's spend less on food." Neither is it fruitful for one spouse to say, "Quit buying all those books." These reductions in your spending plan, just like your goal statements, must be the product of true dialogue. Talk to each other about temporary life-style changes that might enable your long-term financial plan to work for you. At the end of this chapter is an example of how to meet a financial crunch. Perhaps this is where you are already. Don't despair. You really can get there from here.

When Do Savings Become Investments?

If savings are the seeds of investment, it should be apparent that at some point they will need to be planted. See the chapter on investing for a more detailed analysis of the various investment instruments. Here we will explore instead why you will need a variety of accounts to make your many goals simultaneously attainable.

As money begins to accumulate in your savings account, you will need to make periodic withdrawals to establish separate investment instruments for each of your financial goals. Once you achieve your goal of an emergency fund equal to three months of cash flow (see page 36), you won't need to make withdrawals. Simply quit putting new money into the emergency fund. As long as the emergency fund is earning at a rate equal to or greater than the rate of inflation, you should not need to add to it. Make certain, however, that this fund is completely liquid (available) at all times. Your best bet for an emergency fund account is probably a money market fund in which earnings tend to meet or beat the Consumer Price Index while providing full liquidity. Your other savings accounts need to be "spun off" regularly for distribution into a variety of investment "pockets." Of course, this is more work than leaving the money in one place, but there's a good reason why it's worth the effort.

Put a name on each investment. The name should match the goal for which it is committed. For example, your short-term goal might be the purchase of a new car eighteen months from now. You might call this your car account. (I always call mine my Mercedes account even though I've never had a Mercedes. I probably never will have one, but it's a lot more fun to put money into a Mercedes account instead of a Yugo fund!)

It's not enough just to establish a bunch of accounts. Each account should be in an investment instrument appropriate for the goal toward which it's committed and for the frequency of deposits. A certificate of deposit might be a fine investment choice for your Mercedes account as far as the time frame is concerned—eighteen-month C.D.s are readily available. But what about next month or three months from now? You may find that a money market fund or a bond mutual fund is a better investment for this purpose. You'll be able to make additional contributions at any time and can withdraw funds ahead of schedule if you need to.

Sometimes there are other reasons that determine what type of fund is appropriate for an investment account. In addition to time and liquidity requirements, tax considerations also can make a big difference in investment selection. For example, how about your college fund? Here the time frame is likely to be long enough that liquidity will not be an issue, but taxes can erode an otherwise sound plan. Consider a growth-oriented mutual fund instead. The growth builds up tax-deferred and avoids a current tax bite. Zero coupon bonds can be targeted for the time frame your kids will need the money and produce a guaranteed amount you'll know in advance. This can be just what you need if you have a specific financial goal to meet. Some (not all) zero coupon bonds allow you to defer the tax on the increase until maturity. U.S. Series EE Savings Bonds are a popular example of a zero coupon bond.

Consider giving the fund to the child as the teen-age years approach. Remember, even under tax reform's "Kiddie Tax," the first $500 of interest will be tax-free to the child, the next $500 of interest will be taxed at the child's 15% rate, and only earnings beyond this $1,000 threshold will be taxed at your rate. Once the child reaches age fourteen, the entire amount of interest earnings will be taxed at his or her bracket rate, not yours. This strategy can increase the yield of college-oriented investments by nearly a third. Here's how.

Suppose you have accumulated a college fund of $12,500. Invest the money in a certificate of deposit yielding 8% and you will earn $1,000, but you'll get to *keep* only $720 after you pay the 28% income tax. If the child owns the fund, however, the first $500 is tax-free and the next $500 is taxed at 15% ($75), leaving an after-tax yield of $925 on the same investment. When compounded over several years this increased yield can produce dramatic results. Over eight years, for example, the same college fund grows to $19,795 when taxed to you, but reaches $22,554 when in your child's name—a 38% greater yield through the tax-efficiency of this strategy.

When the goal is a long way off, like a retirement fund, try to be specific about what the fund is intended to provide. For clergy this may be a retirement income goal or a retirement home. If it's a retirement home you're investing for, consider investing in real estate in the first place. You'll lock in the right kind of inflation protection because your gains will be related to the real estate market. Since 1970, inflation in the housing sector of the economy has increased at nearly twice the rate of other items in the Consumer Price Index. What this means is that even a good inflation-adjusted investment plan may fall behind the real estate target. Investing in a property now locks in a gain commensurate with your goal's increase. In addition to this inflation protection you get tax-deferral on the gain (see chapter 9 for more on this).

If you're close enough to retirement to know what you want in a retirement home, you may be able to buy it now, rent it to cover the amortization, and permanently avoid tax on the gain in property values. In addition, the favorable tax treatment of rental property creates a situation where investing in a house can produce tax deductions (through depreciation) instead of taxable income.

Now let's recap the basics of your spending plan.
1. Calculate your monthly income.
2. List fixed expenses.

3. Create an emergency fund.
4. Include deferred spending.
5. Adjust variable expenses as necessary to balance the plan.
6. Transfer amounts from deferred spending to individual investments at regular intervals. Each investment will have a name and an investment instrument appropriate for the goal.

How much do you need to put into these savings/investment accounts? That will be determined by your financial goals and time. The longer you have to build up a college fund, the smaller the amount necessary to achieve it. But how can you know how much you need to save now to attain a major goal twenty years from now? Financial planners use a technique called "present value analysis" to determine the monthly payment required to accumulate a desired amount of funds at some future date. You may wish to consult a planner to determine these sums. For about $75 you could purchase a financial function calculator that can do the same calculations for you. The Hewlett-Packard 12-C or the Texas Instruments Business Analyst 54 are relatively inexpensive machines capable of this type of computation. Need $13,000 for a new car in three years? Key in the values—future value = $13,000, time period = 36 months, interest rate (on your money market fund) = 7%—and the monthly deposit required is $325.57! Shooting for a retirement income supplement fund? How much is your goal? If you'll need $50,000 in twenty years, your calculator will tell you that your monthly deposit into retirement income will be $84.89 (if you assume an 8% yield).

Frequently pastors discover that the required amounts are more than the spending plan will allow at this time. Start with a smaller amount and resolve to increase it next year and each year until you achieve the required amount. Be aware that starting with smaller amounts today will increase the future amount you'll need to establish. But get started with something every month.

Facing a Financial Crunch

All of us are going to have crises in our lives. Some will be financial or will create financial stress. There are some financial crises that give us warning and time to prepare. The birth of a child and college expenses are two such examples. There are also those related to accidents, illness, change of employment or no employment. Let's take the easiest first—those financial crises that give us some warning.

By talking to your doctor, hospital, insurance carrier, and other new parents you can get a good idea of how much the new baby will cost. O.K., we know how much we need and how much time we have to get it. Assuming we do not have the necessary money saved for this purpose, we must create a crisis budget.

Perhaps half or more of the amount can be saved through this strategy. Delaying some expenditures, adding dollar-stretching recreation, and simply "doing without" for the sake of the new child may not only work but also feel good.

When the need is clearly before us, there may be instances when that need can be redefined and a refreshing, satisfying solution found. For example, every newborn needs a bed, but perhaps the crib that held fifteen of your kin would have more meaning and would save dollars. Would you "let" the grandparents provide a costly item or two? Most new grandparents would be delighted to assist with items for the grandchild.

This also may be the time to consider a loan from a credit union, bank, or relative. Remember, every lender gets payments of principal and interest each month. If you can't afford to pay this, you can't afford to borrow.

What might have been a financial crisis has become a planned event free from economic stress and worry because you have taken the problem apart and solved it bit by bit.

Sometime, however, you may be hit with a financial sledgehammer! This may come in the form of an accident, illness, loss of income, or unusual circumstance—your "friend" stops paying on a car you co-signed for and the bank comes after you! Whatever variety the problem is, it can usually be spelled l-a-c-k o-f c-a-s-h. In addition to being short of money, you may still be in shock from the cause (accident, loss of trust, etc.). Since we won't think straight once the financial crisis hits, better to do it now while we can work through it.

1. First, you need to do everything you did when you could see the crisis coming.
2. Next, make only necessary expenditures. This time we're talking about basics—food, shelter, and some clothing. Question every dollar, even in these categories. Many parsonage families have large personal phone bills. Outline what you are going to say before you call—or write a letter!
3. Utilize all your benefits—such as insurance. If your problem is an auto accident, have someone in the business look at both your auto and health policies so you can maximize benefits. If you fail to get a second opinion for some medical procedures you may limit your coverage.
4. Call your creditors and refinance or re-negotiate loans. This is a tough one, but ESSENTIAL! It's hard for a pastor to do this in her or his own community, but you are dealing with a crisis. Do this before you are overdue. Such payments will not go away, and you may avoid late fees by securing concessions early on. Would your creditor consider interest only for three months? Phone again when there is any change, and send partial payment if possible.
5. Sell items of worth that you don't value or could manage without. What about that sailboat you only had out once last year? Sell it. Once you get through this crunch you can think about a bigger one. Could you get along with one less car for a year or two? Sure would be nice to save that auto insurance premium, too.

In order for these steps to be effective, we believe the financial crisis should be discussed with your immediate family, including children. Their ideas and cooperation are essential if you are to survive.

Remember, such cash crunches are normal at some point in most families—and you certainly want to be normal. We hope you will follow these suggested steps when your turn comes and that you will emerge from your crisis stronger than before.

BROOM-HILDA By Russell Myers

6

Strategies for Saving

There is a ritual that occurs at nearly every financial planning seminar I conduct. Clergy cluster around me and one question is certain to arise: What's the best place to invest today? I have learned that before I attempt even an equivocal answer I must ask a qualifying question: How much do you have to invest? Answers vary, of course, but it is not uncommon for would-be investors to have less than $2,000. At this point I reply, "You're not ready to begin an investment program. Go home and acquire the savings habit and then we'll talk about it."

I am convinced that virtually every financial plan will be determined by the person's ability to practice a regular, systematic strategy of saving money. Yet some clergy continue to look for miracles or tricks as substitutes for the basic need to put money away today so it will be available tomorrow. Why is this?

Spender or Saver?

People (clergy and laity alike) tend to divide themselves into two basic categories—savers and spenders. Moreover, people seem to know, almost intuitively, which category is theirs. In our seminars we do an exercise which reinforces this. We ask everybody to stand and then we give these instructions: "Everyone go to one of two ends of the room—'savers' to the north end, 'spenders' to the south end. You have 15 seconds.

Go!" It is an amazing sight, but nobody seems to have difficulty identifying at which end he or she belongs. Within just a few seconds everyone is at one end or the other—usually about half at each end!

It's not unusual for couples to find themselves at different ends of the room. He's mingling with the spenders while she's smack-dab in the middle of the savers. The group is then invited to return to their seats (and their spouses) but we notice a significant dialogue going on. Couples frequently testify that they had long felt that they were on different wavelengths regarding savings. Now the reasons for these feelings were evident.

It's important to recognize that there is no qualitative difference between savers and spenders. Neither is better than the other. Savers may feel smugly superior, but they're not. Spenders may think they have more fun, but not really. These are merely two distinctly different personality types—not neuroses to be cured. But it's vital to get in touch with your orientation. Spenders need to establish different savings plans than savers. Things that work perfectly well for savers will just not work if you're a spender. Savers seem to operate from a deep-seated internal motivation, whereas spenders require external motivations to accomplish the same task. If you are a spender married to a saver, you need to have a frank dialogue with your spouse. Without implying any inferiority, you may wish to appoint your spouse the designated saver of the family.

Before you read further, ask yourself frankly, "At which end of the room would I end up? Am I a spender or a saver?" You must get in touch with this crucial issue in order to establish a savings and investment program that is in harmony with your personality.

Fifteen Proven Saving Strategies for Clergy

1. Have your church treasurer deposit part of each paycheck in your savings account (like a payroll deduction). This will require that your bank account be in the same bank as the church's. An alternative is to supply your treasurer with a quantity of bank-by-mail deposit envelopes. We have seldom encountered a church treasurer who was unwilling to perform this assistance.

2. If this is not possible, authorize your bank or savings and loan to automatically transfer a certain amount from checking to savings each month. An alternative to this is the pre-authorized wire transfer to a mutual fund. Most major funds, while establishing minimum deposit requirements for initial contributions, allow monthly transfers of smaller amounts. Even $25 each month can grow substantially when a well-managed mutual fund puts it to work. When the fund is doing well, your money grows. When the fund's value drops, you are able to buy more shares for the same deposit. It's hard to lose with this one.

3. When you get a raise, continue to live on the old amount and deposit the entire raise in savings. (O.K., how about depositing one half the raise?) It's amazing how quickly one can get used to that extra $100 per month. Protect yourself by adjusting your savings each January or whenever your pay is adjusted. Linda, my wife, directs her school's credit union to make extra withholding each September when her new contract commences. I increase my payroll deduction every January.

4. Save any irregular checks like tax refunds, insurance reimbursements, and professional fees. Our boys get allergy shots every week. After the health care plan's deductible requirement has been satisfied, we begin to receive reimbursement checks from the insurance company. Although it is certainly tempting to run out and buy a pizza with this money, we resist. Faithfully deposited, such funds alone could buy you a new car when you retire!

5. Pay off credit cards and save the dollars now spent on interest charges. This may take a little time but can make a big difference in getting from saving to investing. Think of every dollar spent to retire a credit card balance as an investment earning a guaranteed 18%, because that's what it is.

6. If you have mutual funds or stocks, reinvest the dividends. All this requires is notification to the company. Our neighbors will soon be putting a child through college with reinvested stock dividends.

7. When your car loan is finally paid off, wait a year or two before trading and make payments into your savings account. Chances are your car will not drop a great deal in value during

this time because heavy depreciation came early in the loan period. If you have a repair bill during this time, you'll have the money for it already in this savings account. Just think—no more emergency repairs on the Visa bill.

8. Drop your change in a piggy bank each evening and when it's full, give your savings account a "silver lining." We have occasionally put extra banks or canisters in the refrigerator or the cupboard. Whenever I raid the fridge I feel less guilty if I put a quarter or two into my savings piggy bank. I try to pay myself what I would pay in a restaurant for whatever I'm eating. I have a friend who put a large empty industrial acid bottle behind the front door of his house. Each evening as he came in the door he stopped and put his loose change into the bottle. The money was used for Christmas presents.

9. Send money off to an Individual Retirement Account every year. If you don't, you will send a goodly portion of it off to Uncle Sam as taxes. No matter how much your income is, the earnings of your I.R.A. will be tax-deferred until retirement. Don't overlook this strategy. Someone has observed that being able to save money you would not have been able to keep anyway is a painless style of saving. Whether there's pain or not, Uncle Sam is offering to lend you money to save for retirement. And Uncle lets us have the loan absolutely free of interest!

10. Trim your spending by 5%. Look at status items such as name brand sports equipment and designer clothes as places to start. If this works, try another 5%. There are some name brand items that are worth their cost—golf balls, for instance. Other items may be available in comparable quality through house brands or discounts. I have bought most of my clothing from used clothing stores for more than ten years. It's not unusual to find new shirts or shoes in thrift shops for 10% of what you'd pay in the mall—or less. Why are new items in used thrift outlets? The most common reason is that someone bought something that didn't fit. If it fits you, you just got a gift. Remember, put these dollars out of reach, in a savings account, mutual fund, or money market.

11. Let compound interest work for you. Saving early is a painless way of saving more. One thousand dollars deposited at 8% when you are forty-five will become $3,172.17 by the

time you are sixty. If you had deposited that same $1,000 at 8% when you were thirty you would have $10,062.66 by your sixtieth year. Do it early! See what the real costs of procrastination are. See item #15 in this section.

12. Say to yourself and your family that this month we are tithing 10%, saving 10%, and living on 80% of our take-home pay. Then, practice what you have preached. If you increase your giving to 10% or more and are able to tax-defer your 10% for savings, you may find that the 80% that is left is almost as much as you took home before because of the diminished tax bite.

13. A question often asked during our clergy financial seminars is, "How do we get the few dollars you suggest we save each month?" One answer is from professional fees.

Many ministers receive fees for their services at weddings and funerals. In our area one might get $50 for a funeral and $30 to $100 for a wedding. If these checks were sent directly to a savings account, and you averaged $80 per month, your twelve-month total would be $960. This $80 per month compounded at 10% for five years would be $6,195; for ten years, $16,388—from just two such fees per month!

A pastor friend, now retired, saved his fees (and took other steps) for many years and is able to give 50% of his retirement income away!

14. Here is a plan for forced savings. Younger clergy often ask how to discipline themselves to save regularly. Pastors who find themselves to be spenders often need an outside or artificial form of self-discipline. Here's an example from one parsonage family that learned to save after five post-seminary years of failure.

The Spenders (not their real name) had been unable to save. High resolve and occasional bullet-biting had never been sufficient to set aside any meaningful capital. Recognizing their need for external pressure, the Spenders went to their credit union and borrowed $1,000 through a personal note. They agreed to repay the loan at 12.5% with monthly payments of $89.09 for one year. They then took the $1,000 to a bank and purchased a certificate of deposit of $1,000 at 9%. Each month they paid the credit union the $89.09 until, one year later, they had retired the note. At the same time they had a mature C.D. worth $1,093.08.

During the twelve months the Spenders had paid out $1,069.08 to the credit union and had only $24 more to show for it. However, they had learned to save and next year were able to put the same $89 each month away in a savings account. From now on they will earn rather than pay interest. They're still the Spenders, but now they are the savers, too.

We neither endorse nor reject the Spenders' solution. It is true that they had to pay 3.5% more for their note than they earned on their C.D. However, at the end of the year they had nearly $1,100 more than they started out with. Did you?

15. How to save $250 each month. Regular readers of financial publications know that compound interest works best when practiced over long periods of time. Yet, month after month, countless clergy forgo the powerful edge that compounding offers. Of course, every dollar put into your savings/investment account is a dollar you won't be able to spend on pizza, but remember this: every month you wait to begin your savings plan can cost you $250 or more in extra future expense. Here's how.

The following table shows what the required monthly savings deposit must be to amass a retirement fund of $100,000 at age sixty-five. Each example assumes continuous compounding of funds at the prescribed rate. Note that the decision to delay initiating the retirement fund until age fifty required additional savings of $245—$273 per month more than accounts begun at age thirty.

Age	Return on Investment	Monthly Deposit	Future Fund Goal
30	6%	$ 70.19	$100,000
30	7%	55.52	100,000
30	8%	43.59	100,000
40	6%	144.30	100,000
40	7%	123.45	100,000
40	8%	105.15	100,000
50	6%	343.86	100,000
50	7%	315.49	100,000
50	8%	288.99	100,000

Retirement is coming whether you're ready for it or not. Can you really afford to wait another month before making regular contributions to a retirement account?

—— 7 ——

An Introduction to Investing

Once you have acquired the savings habit, something strange will begin to occur—you will be confronted with the need to invest your savings. There is a dramatic difference between these two concepts, and many clergy who are good savers could accomplish much more if they took the time to learn a little basic investment strategy. You don't need to be a Wall Street wheeler-dealer to get the most out of your cash. A little information and the careful creation of a plan consistent with your goals can produce dramatic results. Let's see how the game is played.

While there are seemingly endless variations, investment vehicles fall into three basic categories: cash, bonds, and equities. By cash we mean investments that can be readily converted to cash with no loss of principle at any time. This concept, called liquidity, is found in bank savings accounts, money market accounts, and money market mutual funds. Bonds are actually loans in which the investor agrees to loan funds to a borrower (such as a bank, corporation, or government body) for a period of time in return for the payment of interest. At the end of the stipulated time period, the borrower returns the amount of money originally invested. Examples of bonds are certificates of deposit, treasury bills, bonds and notes, corporate bonds, and municipal bonds. Equities are investments which purchase ownership in property—real estate or corporations. The most common equity investments are real estate properties and corporate stock. Because I will explore real estate strategies in a later chapter, I will limit my discussion of equity investments to corporate stocks.

Understanding Risk

If there were such a thing as a risk-free investment, I would be glad to recommend it to you. There is, unfortunately, no such thing. Every investment has some risk associated with it—that's why investments pay a premium, a return, to compensate the investor for assuming whatever risks are implicit in this particular investment. If you remember only one thing about investing, remember this statement: *Risk and return are related.* The market is wonderfully efficient; the higher the risk, the higher the return. Therefore, when you are presented with two investment opportunities—one with a return significantly higher than the other—take note and recognize that one is riskier than the other one. Of course, you may still elect to invest in the riskier venture, but you will at least know what you're getting into.

Here's a quick comparison of the sorts of risks associated with these common investments.

TYPE OF INVESTMENT	EXAMPLE	RATE OF RETURN	RISK EXPOSURE
1. Cash	Passbook	5.5% (3.2)	Inflation
2. Bond	Insured C.D.	9% (4.2)	Inflation
3. Equity	IBM stock	12% (9.5)	Business Market

Cash investing is represented in this chart with a bank passbook savings account. Today a return of about 5.5% is all you can expect. Assuming that you will invest in an FDIC-insured bank (and not put more than the insured limit of $100,000 in it), where is the risk of this investment? The primary risk is the influence inflation will have on the value of the money. Although the government is willing to guarantee that you will get your money back, there is nothing to insure what the funds will be worth when you withdraw them.

Indeed, for long-term investments, the greatest risk of all is what inflationary forces may do to the worth of invested funds. For example, let's say that you invested $10,000 in a bank savings account paying 5% on January 1, 1970. Over the next twenty years the fund is left undisturbed. Now you need the money to buy a retirement home. How much will the account be worth? Even though the money has been invested at what now seems to be a low return (only 5%), you may be surprised to learn that compound interest has nevertheless increased your $10,000 to a total of $27,015! But what is this really worth? Believe it or not, your $27,015 actually has less buying power than your original $10,000 had twenty years ago! In fact, just to keep pace with the cost of living, your original deposit would have had to increase to $31,974. And this does not take into account the increase in the cost of real estate, which has increased even more. It is clear that even investments you thought to be absolutely safe can have significant risks.

So how about bonds? Historically they pay higher rates than bank passbooks or other cash investments. Does this higher yield indicate a higher level of risk? Yes, it certainly does. Remember: Risk and return are related. So what's the risk? The same inflation risk that is present with cash investments is also present with bonds—even more so now since the period of investment tends to be longer than with cash.

However, in addition to inflation, bonds offer another significant source of risk—interest rate risk. This risk, though commonly overlooked by neophyte investors, is present with every bond type of investment. Remember how bonds work. The investor loans the bond issuer the face value for a stated period of time at a stated interest rate. However, what happens when you want your money back before the bond is mature?

The good news is that nearly all bonds may be sold at any time, even years before the bond matures. The bad news is that the price you'll get for your bond will not necessarily be what you paid for it. You'll receive what the marketplace thinks your bond is worth today, and the primary determinant of bond values is interest rates. Let's take a look at how these bond values "float" with prevailing market rates.

Suppose you have a $10,000 bond that matures in four years

and pays $825 annual interest—8.25% of the face value. Today, however, rates have climbed higher—let's say to 11% for bonds with similar maturities. To sell your bond you will need to make your interest stream competitive with yields available in the marketplace. The only way to do this is to discount your bond's price. The price you'll receive under these conditions will be about $9,000. The bond purchaser will receive an effective "yield-to-maturity" of 11%. Here's how. The buyer will receive: (1) $825 annual interest (9.17% of $9,000) and (2) $10,000 when the bond matures in four years (a $1,000 gain that is guaranteed if the bond is held to maturity), the equivalent of another $250 of income each year. This means that the new investor will be receiving $1,050 each year, the equivalent of 11.7%. Risk in bond investing? You bet.

Stock investments have risk, too. Almost everyone except your friendly broker remembers this. But are stocks really that much riskier than cash or bonds? As we have seen with each of these investment options, it depends on what type of risk you fear. Even supposedly safe investments like passbooks are subject to the perils of inflation, and bonds can sink like a stone during rising interest frenzies. So, "what's the deal" with stock?

Stock is a form of ownership in a company that is publicly traded. This means that you, along with many others, can own a slice of the business—a share. Each share represents a fraction of the value the marketplace places upon the company as a whole. In theory, your fortunes are tied to the performance of the company—as the business prospers, so should you. In reality, however, your immediate return is linked more to what the market thinks about your company's future prospects than to any reality associated with the business. Thus, there are two important risk exposures to stock ownership: business risk and market risk.

Business risk refers to the prospect that the company may experience business reverses. What if the new computers the company makes don't sell? Or what if someone else begins to dominate the computer market and drives down the prices of computer products? Profits for the company would tumble either way and would take the price of the company's stock down with it. To some degree, one can guard against this eventuality through careful stock selection and careful monitoring of the company's quarterly reports. (You may need the assistance of your broker on this.) In the long run, however, business risk is simply one of the risks of stock investments and can never be completely avoided.

Perhaps a more significant risk associated with stock ownership relates to market forces rather than the strength of the individual business. As we noted earlier, the price of a share represents what the market believes it to be worth. This can vary dramatically from any reality-based evaluation. For example, in October 1987 the stock market experienced a wave of panic selling, remembered today as Black Monday, during which the Dow Jones Industrial Average (a commonly used barometer of the entire stock market) plunged 508 points. During this freefall, shares of some corporations dropped $20 or more. Did this indicate that these companies had suddenly become bad businesses or that they would no longer be profitable? Not at all. It merely indicated that the market had changed its view of the value of stock ownership. These $20 declines were simply individual manifestations of the entire trend. So-called market risk, then, refers to the fact that fundamentally sound companies can nevertheless experience price declines whenever market forces drive the price down.

So, every investment—cash, bond, or stock—entails certain risks. Which investment vehicle has the most risk? This question must be answered with another question: Which kind of risk do you mean? If inflation risk is what you want to avoid, stock may very well be the least risky of your investment options. However, if business risk is what you're afraid of, stock would be the last place to park your money.

All of this is fundamental to investment selection as we clarify goals and formulate savings plans. The trick is to match financial goals (see chapter 5) with appropriate investment instruments. A major determinant is the available time frame. Short-term goals, for example, have little risk from inflation, so the primary challenge is to avoid losses from market, interest, or business cycles.

Let's say your goal is to purchase a new car one year from now—a relatively short-term goal. Here the risk is everything but inflation, so you will select something that assures interest with no loss of principal—cash or short-term bonds. In nearly every market the bond will produce higher yields than cash, and since you will hold the bond the full year until maturity, there is no interest-rate risk. Your choice here is clear: a certificate of deposit.

Investment choices are not always so obvious. Perhaps your goal is five years away. What now? Five years is still a relatively brief time span, but inflation can begin to make an impact on yields. Similarly, five years may be sufficient to recover temporary losses from market dips or interest jumps. Do you accept the higher potential yields of stock or prefer to stick to the relative safety of a five-year bond? Remember the fundamental fact of investing—risk and return are related. Look again at the chart that compares the three investment types (page 52) In parentheses beneath the rate of return column are historic average yields over twenty-five year periods, expressed in annual rates. You will note that over time, stock outperforms both cash and bonds by significant margins. With this substantial potential difference in return, the stock investment might look awfully good. But what about periods when the bond yields are up—9% in our example verses 4.2% historically? With a spread between stock and bonds of only 3% rather then 5.3%, the decision is a little tougher.

How to Invest

Even after you have narrowed things down to a single investment choice—cash, bond, or stock—you'll still need to make a critical decision: which company's stock or what bond to buy. Yields on individual securities may vary widely—even among similar types and maturities. A wrong guess can cost you hundreds of dollars. What's a good way to avoid this jeopardy?

I recommend that you not buy individual stocks at all and that you seldom purchase long-maturity bonds. Instead, use the strategy millions of Americans have discovered—invest through mutual funds. A mutual fund is a form of pooled investing. Cash contributed to a mutual fund buys a pro rata share of the fund itself (a closed-end fund) or a share of the fund's assets (an open-end fund). The advantage of a mutual fund is that it provides the small investor with an opportunity to achieve broad diversification without purchasing dozens of separate investments.

However all mutual funds are not alike. In fact, today there are more than 1,100 funds from which to choose. When someone asks "Should I buy a mutual fund?" it's like asking, "Should I buy a car?" The more appropriate question is, "What kind?" Last year Americans bought more than $144 billion worth of mutual funds. Clergy in particular are learning that mutual fund investing can be an effective alternative to individual ownership of stocks and bonds. But, before you take the plunge, here's a quick list of questions to ask prior to making a mutual fund investment.

Question #1—What is the purpose of the fund?

Funds vary widely and dramatically in the purpose to which they are committed. Funds with a particular goal will invest in a particular set of investment instruments.

Among the common categories of funds are aggressive growth, long-term growth, growth and income, balanced, bond, and specialty or sector funds.

Beyond the basic purpose, which might be simply growth, how does the fund intend to achieve the stated objective? Some funds use aggressive "guessing games" like market-timing in which the fund speculates on the direction prices are going to go. These funds are called "timers." When timers are right, they can achieve superior results, but when timers are wrong, the bottom drops out. Other funds may look for small, emerging growth companies—then they're your wagon to the young business's star. Be aware that for every Apple Computer which explodes from nowhere there are a dozen small companies that never make it. You might be wiser to look for funds that focus on corporate earnings, free cash flow, and price/earnings multiples. You don't need to understand any of these concepts as long as you trust the mutual fund manager to understand them.

Question #2—Are the fund's goals consistent with your own?

No matter how effectively a fund works toward its goals, unless your personal goals parallel those goals you may not be well served. Long-term growth funds may sell at a loss if you need to sell in the short-term. Aggressive funds may be much too risky for many of us. Some funds use tax considerations such as capital gains or tax-exempt bonds, which may be inappropriate for lower-income clergy.

A significant issue of interest to clergy is the social implications of mutual funds. Investing in certain types of businesses—gaming, alcohol, tobacco, nuclear weaponry— may be repugnant to many clergy colleagues.

The answer may be investing in a mutual fund with a social conscience such as PAX World Fund. Started by Christian laypersons in 1971, PAX is the first full-scale "social responsibility" fund. PAX invests in renewable energy projects, health care programs, building materials, housing, retail enterprises, pollution control, and leisure. With assets over $25 million, the fund has averaged a 14% return since 1975. (Phone 1-603-431-8022 for details.) Read all material carefully before reaching a decision.

Two other social responsibility funds for your consideration include Calvert Social Investment Fund and Dreyfus Third Century Fund. Calvert offers a "managed growth portfolio" without involvement in certain social issues. (Phone 800-368-2748 for a prospectus.) Dreyfus Third Century (800-645-6561) has a similar investment strategy with the exception of slightly higher liquidity.

The Social Investment Forum, established in 1984, is a small but growing forum for individuals and groups wishing to expand the network of socially responsible investing. Individuals may join the Forum for a $100 membership which entitles you to be put in touch with investment counselors, companies, and financial institutions with social views congruent with yours. In addition, you'll receive notices of professional services offered by fellow members plus information concerning conferences held across the country addressing issues of interest. If the $100 membership is too steep, you may elect a $25 membership which will put your name on the mailing list for professional services. For additional information and a list of social investment vendors, contact Pat Davidson, 711 Atlantic Ave., Boston, MA 02111; 617-423-6655.

Question #3—Is there a load or commission charged on the sale? How much is it and how is it charged?

AN INTRODUCTION TO INVESTING

"Loads" are sales commissions charged on many, but not all, mutual funds. In theory, a good fund will perform well enough that the load is reimbursed. In practice, however, there is often little relationship between performance and whether or not the fund has a load.

If the load is front loaded—charged when deposits are made—any gains are calculated on the balance (deposit minus the load). With some loads as high as 8.5%, you would have to earn an extraordinary return to cancel out the load in the short run.

Here's an example:

$100.00	contribution
− 8.50	(8½% load)
91.50	amount deposited in fund
+ 9.15	10% annual earnings
$100.65	balance at year end
	Net earnings = .65%

Rear loaded funds charge commissions on amounts withdrawn. Rear loads are usually lower than front loads, but remember that they are calculated on higher amounts—the contribution plus any earnings.

For years this argument has raged: Are mutual fund sales commissions (loads) worth the price in terms of increased performance? We have recommended no-load funds for years. Recently, a new study compares both kinds of funds over a fifteen-year period—and guess what? We were right.

The study, released by the Institute for Econometric Research, compared no-load funds with all types of funds over three five-year periods extending from 1971 through 1985. Whereas previous studies had hedged in declaring either group a definitive winner after deducting sales commissions (loads), the Econometric study showed no-loads to be the clear winner.

Over the entire fifteen years of the study, for example, no-load growth funds averaged an annual rate of return of 11.2% compared to only 8.8% for all growth funds. What does this mean? If you had invested $10,000 in the average no-load funds at the beginning of the fifteen years, your account would have grown to $48,900 by the end of the period. The equivalent yield on all growth funds would have been $35,000. In this case, the no-loads would have produced nearly $14,000 in additional yield.

Should you ever pay a mutual fund load charge? Of course—if there are compelling reasons that fit your style and investment objectives. An excellent growth fund with a low front-end load might be entirely consistent with your long-term investment objectives. Be aware, however, that sales agents often recommend loaded funds because of the higher commissions charged. It's a good deal for the agent, but not necessarily for you. Always ask a sales agent what the load is on a mutual fund. As a general rule, front loads are only worth considering for long-term investments, whereas rear loaded funds might be acceptable for short-term objectives in excess of one year.

Question #4—Are the purposes and properties of the fund consistent with your goals and needs?

When you're young you can afford a mistake or two with investments. As you approach retirement, however, it becomes increasingly important to protect your investment from shrinkage. Clergy who are nearing retirement or any other financial goal may be poorly served by aggressive or growth-oriented funds. These funds use strategies which may result in short-term losses. Over the long haul they tend to more than make up for any dips along the way. But what happens when you need the money (for down payment on a retirement house, for example) at precisely the time stocks have taken a nose-dive? Similarly, many funds are extremely interest-sensitive and experience a roller-coaster of ups-and-downs. Should you need your cash when the fund is down, you lose.

Question #5—How can I get my money when I need it?

Your nest egg is about to hatch. You've reached your financial goal and are ready to buy a cottage/car/college education. How easy is it going to be to cash in your chips? Most funds provide toll-free (800) numbers through which you can withdraw portions or all of your invested funds. Black Monday of 1987 proved, however, that toll-free numbers can be chronically busy at precisely the time you want to bail out.

IT WOULD BE JUST OUR LUCK FOR CHURCH TO BE RAPTURED NOW THAT WE'VE FINALLY PUT THE KIDS THROUGH COLLEGE AND PAID OFF THE MORTGAGE.

Another attractive feature of funds with 800 numbers is the opportunity to switch between families of funds. Such "families" are varieties of mutual funds managed by the same company. Such operations allow you to move money instantly from a stock fund into a bond fund by phone. Even though you may never see such transferred funds, for tax purposes the transaction is a sale and may produce a taxable gain.

The Eighth Wonder?

Baron Rothschild once declared that the eighth wonder of the world was compound interest. This dull little nugget is, nevertheless, the keystone of most of our investment strategies, and we would be wise to understand it.

Basically, compound interest is "interest on interest." After a certain amount of interest is earned, it is added to the principal amount, and, in turn, earns additional interest. The result of this phenomenon can be dramatic, indeed.

For example, English astronomer Francis Baily once estimated that a British penny invested at an annual compound rate of 4% at the birth of Christ would have yielded enough gold by 1810 to fill 357 million earths! You don't have to wait that long to see results, however.

Consider a $10,000 investment at 8%. The principal throws off $800 annually ($10,000 × .08 = $800). Over ten years this amounts to earnings of $8,000 ($800 × 10 = $8,000). With annual compounding, however, the total investment is not merely the sum of principal plus simple interest ($10,000 + $8,000), but is the additional earnings of interest on interest. The compounded total investment is now a whopping $21,589!

However, it is not enough to appreciate that compounding is good. You must ask how frequently the compounding is applied. Some banks advertising higher rates will, in fact, pay less interest because they compound less frequently. For example, our $10,000 compounding annually at 8% will grow to $14,693 after five years. If, however, the bank compounded quarterly, the fund would grow to $14,859; weekly compounding would produce $14,914.

Here's a shortcut to using compound interest tables: THE RULE OF 72. This principle calculates the period of time required to double a sum of money at a certain rate. Simply divide 72 by the rate. For example, 72 ÷ 8 = 9 shows that it takes nine years for an 8% investment to double.

A free booklet on this subject is available from the Federal Reserve Bank of New York, Public Information Dept., 33 Liberty St., New York, NY 10045.

8

Individual Retirement Accounts and Tax-Deferred Savings Plans

One of the greatest investment decisions you can make has little to do with picking the right investment vehicle and is, instead, the product of utilizing the right investment contribution plan. This miracle is the genius of investing with pre-tax dollars. The dramatic results of Individual Retirement Accounts, tax-deferred and tax-sheltered pension plans are possible when investment results are not diluted by the bite of income taxes. Let's take a look at how this works.

The principle that enables these tax-deferral strategies to work is based on the concept of deferring income. Today's tax code allows income to be earned while avoiding the receipt of the income until later. This deferral of the receipt of income pushes the tax liability down the road as well. You won't have to declare the income nor pay the taxes due until you begin to take receipt of the money. During this period of deferral you owe none of the taxes that would otherwise be due on the income.

But why is this such a good deal? Some retirement planners have long suggested that deferring income until retirement is smart because income levels (and presumably tax brackets) are lower after retirement. Although there may have been some truth to this concept in the years before tax reform, today's tax brackets hardly favor retirees. The value in deferring income is the time value of money. Taxes owed but deferred until later become, in effect, interest-free loans given us by Uncle Sam.

By deferring these taxes we have access to funds for investment now, with no penalty or interest charged for current use.

For example, suppose that contributing $4,000 to an I.R.A. resulted in the deferral of $1,200 of income taxes. If you did this for only ten years, you would have contributed an extra $12,000 to savings that likely would have gone for taxes instead. Sure, you would eventually have to pay the tax on the money. However, during this ten-year period you also would have earned $6,444 of extra money by investing this $12,000 that otherwise would have gone immediately to Uncle Sam—and earned you zilch!

Remember that an I.R.A. is an individual *retirement* account, so the investment objective is retirement—ordinarily a long-range goal. With this in mind, you will do well to invest with the long haul in mind. The younger you are, the more risk you can tolerate in your portfolio. As you approach the age when you can freely withdraw your money (currently 59½), you will want to safeguard your account by moving into safer harbors. Therefore, don't let anyone pressure you into any particular one-size-fits-all style of investment—your age, cash need schedule, and other personal factors will make too much difference. Similarly, it is important to recognize that I.R.A. rules invalidate many traditional norms of investment. Because there is no current tax liability, there is little need to invest in anything because of the tax consequences of the investment. You wouldn't put tax-exempt municipal bonds in an I.R.A., nor is the appeal of deferred capital gains of much interest when the entire account is tax-deferred anyway. Conversely, the traditional negative concerns of zero-coupon securities are avoided with I.R.A. investing.

Because you can move your I.R.A. around each year, you are not bound to keep it with the initial investment agent. Similarly, you may establish more than one account as long as your annual contributions together do not exceed I.R.A. maximums.

Many have found that I.R.A.s invested in a variety of instruments is a great way to achieve diversification with relative ease. For example, establish one account with a money market fund, another in a growth stock fund, a third in a fixed-income fund, and possibly another in a real estate investment trust. You will have positioned yourself for several different areas of growth and simultaneously reduced your risk.

A word of caution about selection of I.R.A. investments: resist the temptation to move your account into last year's great investment. Trying to chase last year's hot return is probably futile. Many have found out the hard way that last year's winner is seldom a leader the next time around. Don't try to beat the market. Use the asset that is yours—time is on your side.

What Time Can Do to an I.R.A.

You're impressed by what a tax-deferred investment can do, but you're thinking that you'll wait until next year to start. Think again and start today anyway. If you think you can't spare enough to make it worthwhile, at least consider these three factors:

1. $2,000 is the maximum an individual can deduct from I.R.A. contributions annually. You can start an account with a lot less. Something is always better than nothing.

2. The duration of a tax-deferred account is frequently more significant than the amount of annual contributions. For instance, $2,000 contributed for ten years will, of course, require $20,000 in contributions and result in an account of $35,062 (at 10%). Over twenty years, however, only $1,000 need be contributed annually to total $20,000 in deposits, but at 10% the same $20,000 becomes $63,002—a $28,000 difference on the same money is yours if only you start sooner.

3. Because your I.R.A. contribution is tax-deductible, part of your contribution will be money you won't keep anyway— you'll simply pay it in taxes. Uncle Sam is offering you an interest-free loan. This is too good a deal to turn down.

Still need some more persuading? Consider two young clergypersons who elect different I.R.A. strategies. Sharon, at age thirty, begins to put $2,000 annually into an I.R.A. which compounds at 12%. She makes her deposits for only six years and then never adds another dime. Tom, also age thirty, elects to wait until his income is larger. He waits for six years and begins his 12% I.R.A. at precisely the time Sharon quits making contributions to hers. Tom makes $2,000 contributions each of the next twenty-eight years. At age sixty-five Sharon and Tom both retire, and, believe it or not, Sharon has more in her account than Tom, even though Tom contributed 467% as much as Sharon. Sharon's six-year headstart gave her an edge that Tom could equal only if he continued to make contributions for eight more years!

Where to Park Your I.R.A.

You're convinced that you ought to have an Individual Retirement Account. Does it make any difference where your I.R.A. is invested? It sure does! Because I.R.A.s are long-term investments, the return on your account is even more important. On investments covering twenty years or more, even small differentials in rates may result in a dramatic difference in yields.

In our chapter on investing, we showed the historic spreads between yields on cash, bonds, and stocks when continuously invested over twenty-five year periods. Since this historic relationship of stocks outperforming cash investments by nearly three to one has occurred in every twenty-five-year-period since 1924, young clergy would be wise to include stock funds for a major portion of I.R.A. investments. Even middle-aged clergy would do well to have plenty of equity exposure, because that's where the real gains can be made. Growth in the stock market can be so dynamic that even big losses can be recovered over comparatively short periods of time. For example, let's examine what happens to two clergy who adopt differing attitudes toward risk with their I.R.A.s. Ted puts all of his I.R.A. into a growth stock mutual fund which usually produces total returns of 10%. Jane, fearing a market "correction," puts her fund into a money market yielding 8%. The very first year the market drops dramatically—loses 10% of its value—just as Jane had feared. However, Ted sticks to his stock fund strategy, and by the eighth year, has passed Jane's fund—in spite of his early losses.

TAX-DEFERRED SAVINGS PLANS

	Ted	Jane
Beginning Balance	$10,000	$10,000
Year 1	11,000 *	12,800 *
Year 2	14,100 *	15,824 *
Year 3	17,510 *	19,089 *
Year 4	21,261 *	22,616 *
Year 5	25,387 *	26,425 *
Year 6	29,926 *	30,539 *
Year 7	34,918 *	34,982 *
Year 8	40,409 *	39,781 *

* Assumes $2,000 annual contribution

The moral of the story is that the greater return of equities makes the risk of short-term losses worth assuming—if you have time to wait. When your cash needs are less than six years away, you should begin to protect your principal by transferring a portion (perhaps 20% each year) into a more secure fund. When interest rates are rising, transfer into a money market fund. When interest rates are falling, transfer the amount to be withdrawn into a bond fund.

Don't overlook the tremendous long-term differential that small variations can make when compounded. What if Ted and Jane had contributed $2,000 annually to their I.R.A.s and no significant losses had been experienced by either one? Over twenty years Ted's fund would have yielded enough to fund a retirement annuity producing 46% more income than Jane's.

	Ted 10% Equity Fund	Jane 8% Money Market Fund
20 years @	$2,000/year	$2,000/year
Total Contributions	40,000	40,000
Earnings	86,005	58,846
Total Accumulation	126,005	98,846
20 Year Annuity Income	$1,180/mo.	$ 810/mo.

Recognize that the 2% spread between the 10% yield and the 8% yield is really 25% (2% ÷ 8% = 25%). Over the entire twenty years, Ted was earning 25% more than Jane. When it became time to transfer these I.R.A. funds into a retirement annuity, the larger fund was able to purchase an annuity yielding 46% more income ($1,180 = $810 × 146%)!

Tax-Deferred Annuities—Better Than I.R.A.s?

Even though Individual Retirement Accounts are good, clergy have an even more attractive option. The tax-deferred annuity pension fund, often referred to as 403(b) funds, offers several features that are clear advantages over traditional I.R.A.s.

First of all, the tax-deferred annuity is an opportunity for virtually every clergyperson to reduce taxes by planning his or her retirement. This is no longer true for I.R.A.s. High-income clergy (frequently clergy with a working spouse) cannot deduct contributions to an I.R.A. (see the preceding page). But every pastor, irrespective of income, may establish a tax-deferred annuity and defer income taxes on the allowable amounts contributed.

Another plus of the tax-deferred annuity is that you can usually contribute much more than the I.R.A. allows. The critical difference in this limit is that I.R.A. maximums are the same for everyone: $2,000 per year. Tax-deferred annuity contribution limits are based on a percentage of earnings. This distinction can result in substantially higher contribution thresholds—$9,500 on $40,000 of income for example.

Just how much you can defer is determined by a number of individual factors. In general, you may defer up to 25% of your "includable compensation" in any given year. Includable compensation generally refers to cash salary and does not include items like housing/furnishings allowances, church-paid parsonage utilities, or the rental value of the parsonage. (It is important that clergy not rely too heavily on guidance from brochures and other materials intended for lay professionals. The calculation of includable compensation may be quite different for laity and may suggest erroneous limits for clergy contributions).

TAX DEFERRED SAVINGS PLANS

In addition to the general rule of 25% of annual includable compensation, at no time can you have deferred more than 20% of career earnings from the same employment. Rather than add up your earnings from your entire career in the ministry, you may use the current year as a benchmark. Multiply 20% of the current year's includable compensation by the number of years you have been in the plan, subtract all previous year's tax-deferred contributions, and you will have the maximum potential deferral for the current year. Here's what it might look like.

Current year's includable compensation -	$30,000
	× .20
	6,000
Number of years in plan - 14	× 14
Total allowable career contributions	84,000
(Less total contributions to date)	(41,000)
Potential yet-to-be deferred	$43,000

It is important to note that the maximum deferral is limited by these potential restrictions: first, the 25% annual limitation mentioned above; next, a $9,500 annual limit; and finally, the fact that contributions to a denominational pension plan (United Methodist's Ministerial Pension Plan, for example) are themselves part of the tax deferred annuity and reduce the amount that can be added to the allowable total. What this means is that pension payments paid by the church are added to salary in calculating includable compensation, but are subtracted from what might otherwise be an allowable tax-deferred contribution.

If the example above did not include pension payments in the $30,000 includable compensation, these would need to be added. For example, $250 per month would be $3,000 more per year to be included with salary, bringing the includable compensation amount to $33,000. Twenty percent of $33,000 is $6,600. Multiply $6,600 by the fourteen years in the plan, and that increases the total allowable career contributions to

$92,400. Subtract the $41,000 in previous tax-deferred contributions, and subtract the $4,000 previously contributed by the church to your pension account, and the balance will show the maximum yet-to-be deferred. The calculations so far would look like this:

Current year's includable compensation	$33,000
	× .20
	6,600
Number of years in plan - 14	× 14
Total allowable career contributions	92,400
(Less total personal contributions to date)	−(41,000)
	51,400
(Less total church contributions to date)	−(44,000)
Potential yet-to-be-deferred	$ 7,400

Now remember the additional limiting factors. The current year's deferral can't exceed 25% of current income. Twenty-five percent of $33,000 is $8,250, so this threshold is no problem. But remember that the church pension contributions—$3,000—must be subtracted. Once this $3,000 is subtracted from the otherwise allowable $7,400, the most that could then be contributed this year would be $4,400. Note that $4,400 is still more than twice what you could contribute to an I.R.A.

Tax-deferred annuities for clergy are attractive for one additional reason: They reduce your self-employment tax! Unlike the I.R.A., which only reduces income subject to income tax, the T.D.A. reduces income subject to any tax. This means that you defer income tax until you take receipt of the money (generally in retirement or after age 59½. Thus you permanently avoid self-employment taxes on tax-deferred annuity contributions—potentially a savings of hundreds of dollars each year.

To compare an I.R.A. with a 403(b) T.D.A., be sure to evaluate the tax savings from SECA (Self-Employment Contributions Act) as well as income tax.

TAX-DEFERRED SAVINGS PLANS

	I.R.A.	T.D.A.
Current contribution	$2,000	$2,000
Current income tax saving	300	300
Current SECA savings	-0-	306
Total tax savings	$ 300	$ 606

With total tax savings that can be twice as attractive as I.R.A.s, what's the catch with T.D.A.s? There is only one additional step to be taken to gain this substantial advantage. Whereas I.R.A. contributions are deductible as adjustments to income, T.D.A.s must truly be deferred—not received by the taxpayer. This will require all T.D.A. contributions to be sent directly from your church treasurer. To accomplish this, a salary reduction agreement similar to the one below must be endorsed by both church and pastor. These funds are deemed not to have been received for tax reporting purposes.

When You Can't Deduct Your I.R.A.

With the new restrictions on Individual Retirement Accounts, many clergy (particularly those with working spouses) are discovering they can no longer deduct contributions to their I.R.A.s. An attractive alternate is available to clergy with charitable interests.

The deferred payment gift annuity is a strategy through which retirement planning and charitable gift planning come together with attractive advantages. Gift annuities aren't new—they've been around since 1843—but their use in retirement planning has never been more appropriate. In any gift annuity, the donor makes a gift to a charity while retaining life income at pre-established rates. Upon the donor's death, the charity receives the amount still left in the account. In return for this future gift, the donor receives an immediate tax deduction. The income tax write-off is the present value of the actuarially determined remainder interest.

With a deferred payment gift annuity, the donor receives a much larger charitable deduction and higher annuity payments. Here's an example of how the deferred payment gift annuity might work as a retirement planning tool. A

GENERAL BOARD OF PENSIONS
OF THE UNITED METHODIST CHURCH

1200 Davis Street
Evanston, Illinois 60201
(708) 869-4550

Agreement for Contributions to the
Tax-Deferred Annuity Contributions Program

Participant and salary-paying unit (as defined below) agree with one another as follows:

Purpose of This Agreement

This agreement is designed to set forth the terms of participation in the Tax-Deferred Annuity Contributions Program. In making this agreement, the participant agrees to accept a reduction in compensation or to forgo an increase in compensation. In return, the salary-paying unit agrees to contribute the amount of such reduction or waived increase to the Board as contributions to the Tax-Deferred Annuity Contributions Program on behalf of the participant.

Definitions

A. Participant: _____

B. Salary-paying unit: _____

C. Participant's Social Security number: _____

D. Board: The General Board of Pensions of The United Methodist Church, or The Board of Pensions of The United Methodist Church, Incorporated in Illinois, a corporation through which the General Board of Pensions administers its Tax-Deferred Annuity Contributions Program.

E. Tax-Year: The twelve-month period ending on the last day of December of each year.

F. Beginning date of this agreement: _____
   Note: This must be a date subsequent to the date on which this agreement is signed.

G. Term of this agreement: The initial term of this agrement is the period from its beginning date to the end of the current tax year. If the agreement is continued for subsequent terms, each of these shall be an annual period coinciding with the participant's tax year. The term of this agreement shall end on the earliest of the termination of the participant's association with this salary-paying unit, the date of the participant's death, or the date it is otherwise terminated as hereinafter provided.

Terms of This Agreement

1. The participant's annual compensation on the beginning date of this agreement shall be reduced by
   $_____ or _____%, (enter a $ amount or a percentage figure, but not both) according to the following schedule. (The amounts in this schedule are designated as "salary reductions.")

   Initial period (first year) (enter a $ amount or a percentage figure, but not both)

   $_____ or _____% per _____, beginning
                                                    (month, year, etc.)
   _____, 19_____, through _____, 19_____ .

   Subsequent periods (succeeding years) (enter a $ amount or a percentage figure, but not both)

   $_____ or _____% per _____, beginning
                                                    (month, year, etc.)
   _____, 19_____, through _____, 19_____, and thereafter, unless
   a new agreement is completed in accordance with item 3 on the reverse side of this form.

2. If this agreement is still in force at the end of the contract period stated above, it will be automatically renewed for successive tax years until and unless terminated. It may be terminated at any time by mutual agreement or by written notice of election to terminate given by either party to the other. Such notice shall state a termination date that is no less than 30 days after the date notice is given to the other party.

3. A participant and salary-paying unit are permitted to make only one salary-reduction agreement per tax year. If the parties make such agreement and it is allowed to automatically renew for a successive tax year, the automatic renewal will not preclude a new agreement for the current tax year. The prohibition against making more than one agreement during a tax year applies only when the participant makes an affirmative change in the agreement, not where an agreement made in a prior year continues into the next year.

4. The salary-paying unit will forward the amounts of the salary reductions to the Board as contributions to the participant's Tax-Deferred Annuity Contributions Program account. When the salary-paying unit forwards salary reductions to the Board as contributions to the participant's Tax-Deferred Annuity Contributions Program account, the salary-paying unit's obligations to the participant in connection with such payments will be completely fulfilled. The participant is familiar with the Board's Tax-Deferred Annuity Contributions Program and accepts the terms of the program as amended from time to time.

5. The agreement is binding and irrevocable with respect to amounts earned while it is in effect, except that if it terminates because of the participant's death or the termination of employment, any amounts accrued prior to such termination and not forwarded to the Board will be paid by the salary-paying unit to the participant or to the participant's estate.

6. The fact that this agreement continues for a period ending with the participant's tax year does not alter the terms of the participant's employment as to tenure or compensation. The right of the salary-paying unit or the participant to terminate the employment relation or to vary the amount or basis of the participant's compensation that existed without this agreement shall continue to the same extent as though this agreement had not been made.

7. The participant understands that, once funds have been contributed to the plan, the funds are subject to withdrawal by the participant only in the event of one of the following, subject to any revisions or amendments to the Tax-Deferred Annuity Contributions Program:

    a. the time of retirement
    b. the time of termination of conference membership (clergy) or the termination of employment (lay employees)
    c. at the time of disability leave or when a disability benefit is payable
    d. at any time between ages 60 and 70.

Upon the death of the participant, the funds contributed to the plan are payable to the participant's beneficiary(ies) or estate in accordance with the provisions of the plan.

This agreement signed in duplicate by the parties on _____,19_____.

Salary Paying Unit: _____ By: _____
                                                              Name and Title
Participant: _____

1200 Davis Street
Evanston, Illinois 60201
(708) 869-4550

**Billing Request for the Tax-Deferred
Annuity Contributions Program**

Participant Name _____   Conference _____

Participant Number _____   Salary-Paying Unit _____

I have entered into a salary reduction agreement with my salary-paying unit to participate in the Tax-Deferred Annuity Contributions Program. I understand that the effective date of the following billing request cannot be a date which is earlier than the date the salary reduction agreement is executed.

Effective the first day of _____ please bill my salary-paying unit for _____* **per month** for tax-deferred
contributions.   month / year   indicate % or $

This billing arrangement is to terminate on _____. (Do not enter a date on this line if you wish the billing arrangement
to be open-ended. See notes.)   month / day / year

Regarding tax-paid personal contributions to the Ministerial Pension Plan, choose one of the two following options:

☐   Do not bill me for tax-paid personal contributions to the Ministerial Pension Plan.

☐   In addition to the tax-deferred contributions, I wish to be billed for _____ * (indicate % or $) per
    month as tax-paid personal contributions to the Ministerial Pension Plan.

*The total amount billed, including both tax-deferred and personal contributions, must equal at least 3% of your Ministerial Pension Plan contribution base.

Signature of Participant _____ Date _____

Signature & Title of Salary-Paying Unit Official_____ Date _____

Notes:

Participants in the Tax-Deferred Annuity Contributions Program have the responsibility to determine that contributions made on their behalf qualify as tax-deferred and are within the limits specified by the Internal Revenue Code and regulations issued thereunder.

Billing for tax-deferred contributions in the amount listed above will continue until the earlier of
    1. the date you are no longer associated with this salary-paying unit,
    2. the termination date indicated above, if any, or
    3. such time as you provide written notice to the General Board of Pensions that the salary reduction
        agreement has been terminated or the billing amount has been changed.

clergyperson, age forty-eight, discovers that contributions to an I.R.A. would not be deductible. Instead, he establishes a deferred payment gift annuity, naming his church as beneficiary. He contributes $5,000 (unlike I.R.A.s, gift annuities are not limited to $2,000 annually) and receives the following advantages:

1) An immediate charitable income tax deduction of $3,733.61 (about 75% of the $5,000). This results in a current tax savings of $1,045 at the 28% bracket.
2) Annual annuity payments beginning when the clergyperson turns sixty in the amount of $565 (an 11.3% return).
3) Tax exempt income in the annuity of $52.55 resulting in this split of annuity income:

$512.45   ordinary income
$ 52.55   tax exempt income
$565.00   annual annuity

(Note that all I.R.A. income is taxable—principal and interest).

9

Finding and Funding
Retirement Housing

Perhaps the greatest difference between financial planning for clergy and the laity is the matter of providing for housing in retirement. For most lay persons, retirement housing means nothing more than staying where they have been (frequently in a home now completely paid for). Clergy who have lived in parsonages throughout their career discover a completely new set of rules upon retirement. Remember what they told you in your first parish? "Pastor, we know your salary isn't much, but of course we do give you the house." Now the retired pastor discovers that it is all a lie. The house is not yours at all; you've merely had the use of it all these years.

Does it make a real difference to draw a distinction between use and ownership? The name of this game is equity, and it is equity that clergy usually lack when retirement beckons. The retirement life-styles of a clergyperson and their lay neighbors may be dramatically different—even if their pensions were identical—if the pastor must pay $600 per month in rent while the neighbor enjoys a paid-for home.

Clearly, the answer to this dilemma is to plan *now* for your retirement housing needs. Whether your retirement home will be a three-bedroom ranch, a cottage on a lake, or a high-rise apartment is not the focus of our discussion here. What really matters is to have the money for your retirement housing needs, whatever they may be.

How Much Will You Need?

In one regard, clergy and laity have the same challenge—the purchase of a home is usually the largest financial transaction anyone ever makes. Because of the size of this financial goal, great care should be taken to establish a realistic target.

How much will you need for housing in retirement? The issue depends upon what kind of housing you'll require, what it costs now, and how long it will be before you need it for housing purposes. The effect of time and inflation is never so evident as when we contemplate future costs of real estate. Today's $75,000 house will likely cost $200,000 twenty years from now, even if real estate prices increase only at a moderate 5% pace each year. (If real estate inflation averaged 10% over the same period, the price would grow to $500,000!)

Does this mean you'll need to save $10,000 each year to amass $200,000 twenty years from now? Not at all. Remember the genius of compound interest. Recognize as well the impact of a basic principle of retirement planning for clergy—the effect of leverage.

What is Leverage?

Just as a lever is a tool to increase the capacity for lifting, leverage is a tool for increasing the economic impact of certain forces. Real estate is the most common example of the influence of leverage on savings strategy. Saving toward the goal of a retirement home is hard enough without the frustration of watching the cost soar faster than our savings accumulate. Why is this? The effect of leverage is that the amount of today's housing price requires a much smaller percentage increase to grow by a certain figure than your savings will require. Why? Because the house's price begins at a larger figure. Here's an example of the influence of leverage.

If you have $10,000 in your savings account earmarked for retirement housing, you will earn $800 this year on an 8% investment. Meanwhile, the price of your retirement home, although increasing at a lower rate, just went up $3,750 ($75,000 × 5% = $3,750)! You will need to save $250 a month just to stay even—and you're still $65,000 short of your goal.

How can you cope with the influence of such leverage? One way is to make retirement housing a priority early in your career and to put your savings into long-term investments that can grow faster than the price of your retirement home. If you could accumulate as little as $10,000 by the time you turn thirty-five, that amount could almost catch up to the future price of a $75,000 house by the time you turn sixty-five—if you could achieve a continual return of 12% compounded. Although this is an aggressive investment goal, several excellent growth mutual funds achieve a 12% average return on a regular basis.

Use Leverage Yourself

Perhaps a better way to fight the influence of leverage is to use it yourself. For example, what if you invested your long-term money in real estate? For a down payment of 20%, you could achieve a return equal to five times the increase in the price of the house. How? Because your investment is only one-fifth the cost of the house while your return is 100% of the increase. Here's what it might look like.

$10,000 down payment

$50,000 house
+ 2,500 increase in value at 5%

$52,500

$$\frac{\$ 2,500 \text{ net gain}}{\$10,000 \text{ investment}} = 25\% \text{ return on investment}$$

Of course, you will have to make payments of principal and interest on the borrowed money, which enables you to achieve your leverage. These costs, along with other costs of ownership such as taxes, insurance, and up-keep, frequently negate the value of the leverage you've achieved. That's why many pastors choose to achieve property leverage through rental or income property.

If you could receive payments from a tenant to help cover your mortgage expenses, then leverage could really work for you. The chart below illustrates how a rental property can enable leverage to increase the return on a $50,000 single-family house from 5% to an effective rate of 17.3% over ten years. Notice how, with virtually no additional out-of-pocket expenses, your initial down payment of $10,000 grows to an equity of $49,306 after ten years—a compound return of 17.3% annually—while the market value of the house has only increased 5% each year.

THE EFFECT OF LEVERAGE

Assumptions:
    $10,000 to invest
    Single house $50,000
               – 10,000 down payment

               $40,000 mortgage/land contract at 11%

    Annual payments $4,956
    Taxes   1,200
    Insurance, etc.   800
    Total costs $6,956
    Rent @ $500 $6,000
              ($ 956) Negative cash flow for Year #1

Year	Equity	Costs	Rents	Cash flow
2	$15,680	$7,000	$6,300	$ (700)
3	19,052	7,056	6,615	(441)
4	22,630	7,161	6,945	(216)
5	26,428	7,272	7,292	20
6	30,462	7,387	7,656	269
7	34,747	7,508	8,038	530
8	39,303	7,635	8,440	805
9	44,148	7,770	8,862	1,092
10	49,306	7,910	9,305	1,395

        Aggregate cash flow $ 1,798
        Market value of house $81,445

Should You Become a Landlord?

Does this suggest that all clergy ought to own income property? Not at all. There are many other considerations to evaluate before you take the plunge into rental property. Your personality, your handyperson skills, your risk tolerance—each of these will influence whether you're cut out to manage rental property.

What would you do if a tenant was late with a rent payment or refused to pay? Do you have the kind of personality that would allow you to be forceful and businesslike in these circumstances, or would you tend to melt under pressure? Many clergy have developed such empathy for others that it is difficult for them to deal in a businesslike manner with difficult persons. Don't despair. Step back and let your capable spouse manage your rental property. If this is not possible, consider a property management service to act as your agent. For a fee of about 15% of the rent, the agent will perform a variety of tasks to keep your rental operation running smoothly. Is such an expense worth it? If it makes the difference between using leverage or giving up, it may be worth much more than the modest charges for professional management. Be aware, however, that the additional cost must be factored into the equation in evaluating total return. In our example above, the extra expense of the agent would result in a negative cash flow (more money going out than coming in) for each of the ten years. Instead of a positive cash flow of $1,798, management charges result in a negative cash flow of $9,519. In this case, the same money contributed to a good mutual fund would have achieved the same results. (Your $10,000 down payment plus the annual negative cash flow contributed to a mutual fund earning 10% would grow to $43,572 in ten years—with none of the problems of the rental business.)

You Don't Need to Be a Landlord to Own Property

If you decide that owning a duplex or other income property is not for you, does that mean that you must wait to get into the real estate market? Not at all. Now may be the best time to buy, even if you must pay for it with your own money.

Just like an I.R.A. or similar retirement instrument, real estate may be a powerful tax shelter as well as an investment vehicle. As long as the property qualifies as your second residence, you may deduct all mortgage interest and property tax expenses. During the early years of property ownership, this enables you to deduct nearly all your real estate expenses. Unlike the I.R.A., there is no limit to your deduction. Here's how it might look.

Purchase of resort cottage	$50,000	
	− 10,000	down payment
	40,000	mortgage at 11%
First year mortgage payments	4,956	
First year mortgage interest deduction	(4,400)	
Property taxes (all deductible)	(1,200)	
Total first year expenses	6,156	
Total first year deductions	5,600	
First year tax savings (at 28%)	1,568	
Net first year expenses	4,588	
($6,156 − $1,568 = $4,588)		

With annual net expenses of nearly $5,000, you can see that investing in real estate may not be the right vehicle for everyone. The same money invested otherwise would probably earn more. Nevertheless, there are at least four reasons why many clergy prefer property ownership as a strategy for providing their retirement home.

1. Investing in a cottage or resort property provides an asset you can enjoy while it grows in value. Although mutual funds may be enjoyable to own, they aren't much fun to "play with." A cottage, on the other hand, offers a current benefit. Without regard to whether or not the costs of cottage-ownership compare favorably to hotel prices, a vacation spent at your very own place can be a satisfying experience.

2. Investing in a cottage or getaway home provides a sense of roots. The psychic value of owning *something* should not be underestimated. Many are the clergy who testify that the ordeal of the parsonage is bearable only because of the satisfaction from occasionally retreating to one's own place.

3. Investing in real estate means that the return you'll make on your investment will approximate the increase in cost of your retirement home. Even though real property often increases in price at a rate substantially below other investments, prices sometimes skyrocket while other investments languish. Inflationary cycles are particularly vicious in their effects—stocks plunge while real estate soars. Owning a real estate investment of virtually any residential variety provides a hedge against the future price of your retirement home.

4. Your real estate investment may produce tax-advantaged results. While you own your property, the increase in value accumulates tax-deferred. Unlike C.D.s and many other investment instruments in which you pay taxes as you go, real estate defers the gain until you sell. Even then you may avoid the tax bite in some circumstances.

For example, upon retirement, move into the cottage (or other property) and establish it as your personal residence. Should you sell the property, you may roll over any capital gain into another property—your retirement home (IRC Section 1034). After age fifty-five, you may permanently avoid paying tax on up to $125,000 of gain on a personal residence that you have owned and occupied for any three of the preceding five years (IRC Section 121).

10

Saving on Auto Expenses

Until you buy your first house, an automobile is likely to be the biggest purchase you'll ever make. With the price of an average new car now in excess of $14,000, the stakes are high; however, the scale of these numbers suggests a tremendous opportunity for savings if we learn a few of the tricks of the trade.

In this chapter we will explore a variety of strategies to save money on getting from point A to point B. We'll look at ways to save in acquiring, operating, financing, and disposing of your cars. Readers of *Clergy Finance Letter* frequently write to tell us how these strategies have saved them hundreds of dollars. Perhaps your savings will be similar.

Cost-Per-Mile

When preachers get together, one of the constant topics of discussion is bragging/griping about their car costs. One preacher crows about her great mileage, while another laments the low resale value of his two-year-old car. Someone speaks optimistically about hoping to roll over 100,000 miles, while another tells a sad tale about tires. But none of these stories addresses the real issue. Fundamental to any automobile decision is the understanding that the only true measure of auto expense is cost-per-mile. No matter what the price of a car or what the miles-per-gallon experience, the only thing that really counts is what total costs are divided by total miles driven—cost-per-mile.

Many of the traditional car expense mistakes clergy make are based on a failure to appreciate the bottom-line reality of cost-per-mile. A young pastor is seduced into buying a new car he can't afford because of misleading claims about the increased mileage to be produced by the new vehicle. A middle-aged pastor gamely hangs on to a relic that seems to spend more time on a hydraulic lift than on pastoral calls—all the while thinking this clunker is saving money. Another clergyperson trades off by financing for sixty months for "only another $75 per month." Each pastor has missed the point: the true cost of the car is not the gas, the price of the vehicle, or even the monthly payments. True cost is always cost-per-mile.

The IRS currently says it costs 26 cents per mile to operate a late model car. The Department of Transportation says it's really 38 cents, while the Hertz Corporation says it's more like 51 cents. Which figures can you believe? Probably none of these analyses represents your actual experience. You'll have to do your own calculations.

But let's look at what others have found and how they reached their conclusions. An independent cost analysis firm recently published these cost projections for two common vehicle categories. Category A includes economy cars like Chevrolet Cavalier and Plymouth Reliant LE. Category B includes mid-size cars like Chevrolet Celebrity, Olds Ciera, Buick Century, Ford Taurus, and Chrysler LeBaron. Costs are broken down into fixed costs of ownership and variable operating cost—each in per-mile figures.

Category A—per mile
Operating Cost Standards

Fuel (No-lead)	4.24 cents
Maintenance	1.48 cents
Tires	.63 cents

Ownership Cost Standards

Insurance	4.66 cents
Depreciation	14.17 cents
Finance expenses	2.5 cents

Total cost-per-mile	27.68 cents

SAVING ON AUTO EXPENSES

Category B—per mile

Operating Cost Standards

Fuel (No-lead)	4.78 cents
Maintenance	1.63 cents
Tires	.69 cents

Ownership Cost Standards

Insurance	5.20 cents
Depreciation	15.03 cents
Finance expenses	3.15 cents

Total cost-per-mile	30.48 cents

In each of these examples, the assumption was that the vehicle was used 20,000 miles per year. Depreciation was figured using the straight line method. For tax purposes, you will need to depreciate using new MACRS tables and five-year recovery periods (which really take six years). Nevertheless, these figures show that the actual expenses of even economy cars are more than the IRS would have you believe.

However, each of these figures is based on a new car. What if you choose to drive a used car? Although it is reasonable to assume that there will be additional maintenance and up-keep expenses, there is a period when repair costs are not high and yet depreciation expenses are low. According to the Hertz people, a used car that is two to three years old costs up to 40% less to drive than comparable new vehicles. In fact, on some models, the differential is even greater. In one case, the difference between driving a new compact model and a two-year-old car just like it was a whopping 88%!

Before you run off to the showroom to acquire that shiny new set of wheels, at least consider what the difference in cost-per-mile is likely to be for the new one. Go ahead and calculate reduced repair and maintenance costs plus likely savings in gas consumption, but recognize the big increase in depreciation plus the probability of greater insurance premiums. In some parts of the country, insurance is a major variable in the equation. In the Los Angeles area, for instance, the cost of insuring a new compact car can be nearly $1,000 higher than comparable coverage of a similar three-year-old model.

A New Car Buying Strategy*

If you intend to buy a new car soon, let's talk!

Careful preparation can help you save several hundred dollars on this single purchase, and still allow you to have the car of your dreams.

Select the make and model car you want to buy. Kick the tires, take a test drive, and check the repair and maintenance records in *Consumer Reports* magazine. Make sure the price is affordable for you. Tell the salesperson you will return when your price list arrives.

Order the new car buying package from *Consumer Reports* (P.O. Box 8005, Novi, MI 48050). State the make and model. The cost of this package is $10 for one model and $18 for two.

They will send you a print-out showing dealer cost and suggested retail on the basic car and all options. Also included is a step-by-step buying strategy, which we have personally tested.

When the packet arrives, use their percentages to figure out what your first counter offer will be and what your final target amount will be (plus taxes and plates).

Before leaving for the showroom, assemble the following:

1. A paper to hand the salesperson listing the model and all options you have selected.
2. A similar list to which you have added the dealer and retail price for each item.
3. The information from *Consumer Reports*.
4. Your checkbook.

Now, phone ahead to make sure your salesperson is in. Tell him or her that your material has arrived and that you are ready to discuss a purchase.

---

*Charles Fry contributed material for this entry.

Showroom—Here We Come!

Meet your salesperson and place your open folder containing the above items on his or her desk.

Give the salesperson your first list (no prices), telling him or her that your price list has arrived and that you are prepared to buy or to shop elsewhere, depending on price.

Indicate further that you don't need an explanation of the figures listed on one or more stickers appearing on new car windows. You simply want to know how much their firm needs to cover their costs and to make a fair profit. This can then be added to the dealer's cost (which you have figures on the second sheet in your open folder) to determine the purchase price.

Now, wait—through small talk, positioning, and excuses. Keep insisting that the salesperson give you their best price.

Your salesperson may play the "check with my sales manager" game. Continue to wait. Since you expect to save many dollars, the wait may be a good investment.

Finally, your salesperson will write a single figure on a slip of paper and move it across the desk so the CIA and KGB can't see it over your shoulder!

Next, ask questions so you are sure you know what the figure covers. "Are all my options included?" "What about transportation, taxes, and licenses?" (Usually taxes and licenses are added later.)

Your Turn

It is time to respond to the offer. Let's say the offer is $500 above your counter offer and $300 from your target. Simply state that you are pleased with the offer, but that you are $500 from having a deal. Then wait quietly for a response.

If there is no willingness to deal, thank the salesperson for the time spent and move on to the next dealer. You are in charge. You do not have to buy a particular car from a particular dealer.

No doubt there will be checking with the sales manager, expressions of pain, and an offer close enough to your target that you can accept it.

As the sales agreement is being drawn, you should write the following on it: "The full deposit will be refunded if delivery terms cannot be met."

One more thing. Write on the *back* of your deposit check (not the front) the purpose of the check and the car model. If necessary, a court of law would agree as to the specific purpose of that payment.

You are not through yet! Now they will try to sell you several hundred dollars of added services you don't need. Resist! Resist! We suggest a polite but firm no thank you to each of these add-ons.

What About Our Trade-in?

Don't even talk about your present car while negotiating for your new one. It will only complicate the deal. When the price is set for the new car, have the dealer establish the (wholesale) value of your car. You may be able to sell it through a newspaper ad for a couple hundred more. Be sure and reserve that right.

When buying your new car:

1. Take your time and make most of your decisions *away* from the showroom.
2. Get the facts on costs. *Consumer Reports* (see beginning of chapter) is an excellent source for this information.
3. Be prepared to say no to heavy sales pressure. A common gimmick is called "lowballing." The sales agent readily agrees to your offer only to have the deal stalled by the sales manager. The agent preys on your anxiousness to close the deal.
4. Do your own math and understand it; otherwise don't base your deal on it.

We know pastors who have saved at least $500 through this exercise. Maybe you can save even more!

Question: Is leasing for you?

Answer: Yes—if it (1) saves you money, (2) provides a more dependable, late-model car, and (3) saves you time and hassle when buying and selling.

Question: When is it better not to lease?

Answer: When one or more of the following applies.

1. You can own for less money.

2. You plan to drive the car 12,000 miles or less per year and keep it in ship-shape condition.

3. You love to trade when hit by car fever.

4. You can't figure out a good place to invest the capital that you now have tied up by owning.

Question: What factors could make leasing advantageous?

Answer: 1. High mileage. Persons driving over 15,000 or 20,000 miles per year should consider leasing. Although most leases are set at 12,000 or 15,000 miles, the cost of extra miles may be less than your cost of owning. An extra 5,000 at .06 would be only $300.

2. Free capital for other investments. If you need cash to make a down payment on a highly leveraged income property or to help a son or daughter through the last (not the first) semester of college, then leasing could free up funds you now have invested in your car.

3. You want to drive a newer, dependable car and plan to keep it two, three, or four years. This may save you hours in car day-dreaming.

Question: What can the leasing company do better than I can?

Answer: 1. Purchase cars at fleet rates.

2. Borrow money at a lower rate to finance the car (there are exceptions—you may have a less expensive source).

3. The dealer usually can get rid of the used car faster.

Signing the Lease

Make sure your lease is the closed-end type. According to this plan, you simply turn in your car at the end of the agreed time. Payments are limited to one month in advance (like rent security), one payment per month, and any agreed on amount for miles-over-maximum (seven or eight cents is reasonable, five or less is a gift!).

In our opinion, you should not sign any other type of lease than this except under *very* special circumstances, such as greatly reduced monthly payments. Be sure to shop. Some leasing companies can get you almost any car made. We prefer a new car dealer with a good service department.

At the time of signing, secure a guaranteed purchase price for the car (at lease end). Have your dealer write the following across the bottom of your lease (both copies): "At the end of this lease we agree to sell the car described above for a total of $_____." (Signed and dated.) This phrase can save you hundreds of dollars if:

1. The cost of cars has risen and you decide to buy the leased car.
2. You have run up excessive mileage and decide to buy rather than pay hundreds for the extra miles.
3. You can line up a buyer who will buy your leased car when your next leased unit arrives. (A colleague made $500 one day by this method.)

Consider including these options in your lease:

Insurance—especially if the age of your family results in a high rate with your regular company.

Full maintenance—if you drive many miles and the dealer's fee is low.

Remember, your lease should be the closed-end type and the end-of-lease-purchase-price should be written across the bottom.

Leasing and Taxes

Business travel expenses, including leasing costs, are deductible on your federal income tax return. These factors may swing the bottom line in favor of leasing your business car. Such tax savings are not available on personal travel.

Alternatives to Leasing

Leasing may not be for you. Without buying a new car or heading for Honest John's Used Car Lot, how can we meet our transportation needs?

1. Buy a car that has already been leased. Let a leasing dealer know what you want. They can check and tell you when such a car will be turned in and its approximate price. Then you wait. Clergy colleagues have bought several such one-year-old cars with 8,000—10,000 miles, thus avoiding high first-year depreciation.

2. Buy a factory official's car by letting your dealer know what you want. Then wait. The car may have from 3,000 to 8,000 miles on it and may be three months to a year from the assembly line. So it's not your color—adjust!

3. Most school districts have several driver education cars. Inquire of the business manager what dealer provides them or where the board of education trades. Get your name on a list—then wait.

4. Let your friends know you are looking for a low mileage used car. Share the model and year with them. Then write the same information on several three by five inch cards and post them on supermarket bulletin boards. Then wait. Have a mechanic check out any car you buy in this manner. Be sure to haggle over price or you will risk insulting the seller who had planned to come down several hundred dollars! Try to buy with your head as well as your heart. Car fever can set in quickly just because the sun is shining and the car is red!

If none of the above works for you, be careful when visiting Honest John's Used Car Lot!

When You Finance Your Car

Don't Drive Upside Down!

No, this isn't an auto safety notice. Upside down refers to a common condition in auto financing in which the car turns out to be worth less than the amount still owed to the lender. More than common, this condition is almost universal as most new cars lose up to 25% of their value as soon as they're driven off the lot. This is nothing new.

What is new are the increasingly long periods where the upside-down condition continues. Back in the days when auto loans were only twenty-four to thirty-six months in duration, the upside-down condition was temporary, lasting only six to eleven months. Today, however, the average new car costs $14,000, and, not surprisingly, buyers are electing to stretch out their payments for five years or more. More than 70% of the new car contracts financed through both Ford Motor Credit and General Motors Acceptance Corporation extend through five or more years.

Electing the sixty-month loan can reduce the monthly payments by more than $100 (compared with a thirty-six month loan). However, the down side is that you drive upside down 3½ times as long. With five-year financing, you will owe more than the car is worth for more than three years.

The problem gets particularly tough when you decide to trade your car in before it's paid for. After all, just because you've decided to finance the car over five years doesn't mean you want to keep the thing that long. But when you check out a trade-in, you discover, after subtracting the outstanding balance on your old car, that you have only $600 to apply as a down payment on the new vehicle.

What do you do now? Resist the temptation to do what the dealer suggests—to finance for even longer with a low down payment. Such financing results in the equivalent of a lease arrangement in which you'll hardly ever reach positive equity.

Consider keeping the car until it's paid for. Yes, this may require additional repair expenses. Consider, then, the wages of past sins. Finally, resolve to avoid this problem in the future. Plan now to make a larger down payment, to finance for no more than forty-eight months.

Term of Loan	36 Months	48 Months	60 Months	72 Months
Monthly payment on $11,500 loan	$384	$305	$258	$227
Number of payments needed to reach positive equity	11	25	37	51

11

Risk Management—
Choosing the Right Insurance Plan

Insurance is that rare situation in which it is possible to have more for less. Yes, if you know how to select the right insurance product, it is possible today to increase the amount of your coverage while simultaneously reducing the cost of coverage. Done with magic, you say? No, it's really nothing more than understanding how insurance works and selecting products that give you the best value. Let's look at ways you can get the protection you need and still live within your spending plan.

Understanding Risk Management

Risk management is today's term for describing the combination of strategies and products that enable us to live in an uncertain world without extreme risk exposure. Sometimes the best risk management is free. For example, when a chain-smoker "kicks the habit," he or she is practicing a risk management strategy that saves money. Other common measures of managing risk include removing ice from the sidewalk, limiting your sixteen-year-old's use of the family car, and regular exercise. Each of these strategies reduces risk by addressing its cause.

However, some risks simply cannot be eliminated; they must be faced. Insurance is a common tool for reducing certain risks. Insurance shifts the economic burden of uncertainty, in whole or in part, to the company underwriting the policy. A loss would trigger a payment (what underwriters call indemnification) to the insured. Although this payment does not eliminate the loss, it at least reduces the economic impact of it.

Lesson #1

The first thing to recognize about insurance, therefore, is that insurance can solve only problems that have financial solutions. Money cannot bring back a dead child, nor can it replace the irreplaceable. It can only provide a payment upon the occurrence of some event.

What this lesson implies is that insuring the lives of children, retirees, or many non-working spouses is seldom a good idea. Unless funds will be required to replace services currently rendered by the spouse—child care, for example—an insurance settlement will solve no problem, and, in our judgment, is an unnecessary expense.

Lesson #2

Buy only the insurance you require. When you go to the supermarket for a pound of hamburger, you don't buy ten pounds just because someone wants to sell you ten pounds, do you? Of course not. Yet, a major error commonly made by clergy is allowing an agent (salesperson) to dictate what insurance coverage (and cost!) you should select. Resist. Make up your own mind about what you need and shop for value.

Lesson #3

Prioritize your total insurance requirements and allocate your available funds accordingly. For example, an absolute necessity is automobile insurance. That should be acquired first. Next might come homeowner's or renter's insurance for your furnishings and other possessions. (Be certain to cover your professional equipment, such as your library, that may be housed in the church. You will likely discover that the church's policy does not cover such items.)

What next? Before you consider life insurance, ask yourself what risk you're facing that is more likely than premature death. If you are under age fifty-five, the risk of disability is several times more likely than that of death. (See the section They Call It Living Death in this chapter.)

What about life insurance? Most persons have the wrong amount. Younger pastors commonly have too little, while older clergy frequently carry too much. How can you know how much is right for you? Beware of simple formulas such as "five times your salary." Although these multiples offer a quick target for the salesperson to utilize, they seldom address the real issue—how to know how much you really need. Remember Lesson #1—insurance can solve only problems with financial solutions. What financial problems would your death (or the death of your spouse) create? Loss of income would create needs for living expenses, final (burial) expenses, and funds for future goals such as college or retirement housing. Life insurance is one method of solving the economic dilemmas created by a death.

Below is a diagram recommended by the College For Financial Planning for use in selecting appropriate life insurance products. You'll note that it is much more complex than "five times your salary," but it gives the entire process necessary to make certain that you are addressing the right issues.

Lesson #4

Save money by avoiding or sharing risks. A simple way to save on insurance purchases is to assume some of the risk yourself and purchase only the coverage that you can't afford to assume. Deductibles are a form of shared risk. You agree to pay the first level of loss, and the insurance carrier covers the rest.

When was the last time you increased the deductibles on your auto or parsonage contents policies? If you're still carrying $100 deductible, you haven't adjusted for fifteen years of inflation. In the early seventies such coverage was typical, but since 1970, inflation has increased the cost of everything to more than 300% of 1970 levels. Simply increasing your deductibles on your car and furnishings to $250 could save you $100 or more each year—and your risk

THE LIFE INSURANCE SELECTION PROCESS

Part 1

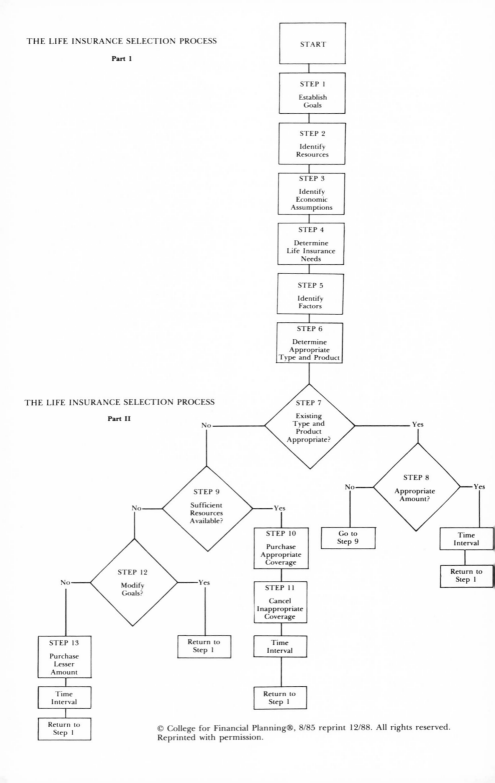

THE LIFE INSURANCE SELECTION PROCESS

Part II

expense would be no worse than it was years ago at the $100 level.

Lesson #5

Insurance is seldom a great savings or investment instrument. Although it is possible for life insurance products to accomplish part of these aims, life insurance has another purpose.

Buy term life insurance and invest additional funds in a true investment such as a mutual fund. Yes, it is true that whole life and other cash value policies provide a form of forced savings. However, if you require external motivation to save—and most spenders do—there are plenty of other methods available.

Certainly, there may be times when something other than pure term insurance is attractive. Beware, however, of the allure of computer print-outs projecting huge cash value accumulations. Sure, $1,000 a year for thirty years can accumulate a lot of money at 9%. But can the accumulated build-up in a life insurance policy really be expected to grow at 9% over the entire time? Probably not. On the other hand, if you have thirty years to invest funds, why not put the difference between whole life and term into a stock mutual fund and profit from the potential for high returns when the market soars?

Lesson #6

Protect yourself against the modern world. In today's world, people sue other people. Is that any surprise? Of course not, but are you adequately protected against the inevitability of liability litigation? Perhaps the thing to do with premiums saved on your auto coverage by increasing the deductible is to spend them on an increased liability policy. If all you have is the customary $100,000, you are hardly protected. Get a minimum of $250,000. While you're at it, check into the possibility of obtaining an umbrella liability policy which protects you from any liability in excess of your current coverage. For approximately $125, you can pick up an additional $1 million of coverage. Compare rates, but note that many companies will only offer this coverage to current holders of their other insurance products.

Facing and managing risk is an absolutely vital part of the financial planning process, but if you know the rules and buy what you need (and only what you need), you can protect yourself and your family.

They Call It Living Death

Remember when the heroine in the melodrama was threatened with "a fate worse than death"? Well, there is something threatening many clergy that may be worse than death. They call it permanent disability.

Permanent total disability, often referred to as living death, may well be the most serious economic peril faced by clergy today. For example, for as many as 30% of United Methodist pastors, this risk is largely uninsured.

Not all clergy share this jeopardy, thankfully. Many are covered jointly by Social Security and their denominational disability insurance plan. Together these two programs coordinate to replace as much as two-thirds of the pastor's former earnings. Whereas it is our view that even two-thirds of one's former income is probably inadequate (especially when housing must suddenly be provided), the greater concern is for a substantial minority who will be forced to exist on less than half their working incomes.

This group of at risk clergy is made up of those pastors who have exempted themselves from Social Security (opted out) and who may not be eligible for Social Security disability benefits. It is important to understand that such pastors may be eligible for retirement benefits from Social Security (through previously covered employment) and still be ineligible for disability payments.

Persons who have earned forty or more quarters of Social Security benefits are considered fully insured and will receive pension benefits from Social Security upon retirement. To receive disability payments, however, the worker must also be currently insured under a separate formula. Clergy over age thirty-one would need at least twenty quarters of Social

Security coverage in the last ten years to be considered currently insured. Clergy with less than the twenty quarters requirement could receive no disability benefits from Social Security and would be dependent solely upon their denominational disability insurance plan. For example, benefits equal to 40% of the denominational average compensation (DAC). For 1989 this would be $10,313 ($25,783 DAC × .50 = $10,313).

Clergy who discover they are not eligible for Social Security disability benefits should obtain disability insurance through an individual policy. In most cases, it is worth the extra cost to get a more liberal "own occupation" coverage that will not require you to become a truck driver if you permanently lose your voice, for example.

Life with a permanent disability is tragic enough without the prospect of living on $10,000 a year. Check your coverage now and avoid this fate that may truly be worse than death.

12

Planning
Your Compensation
Package

The great labor leader Samuel Gompers was once asked, "What does labor really want?" He replied somewhat tersely, "More!" Some clergy, presumably are disciples of Gompers and believe that more money would solve their economic problems. In some cases, this has led colleagues to leave our profession for the greener pastures of secular employment. Other pastors, however, have learned that substantial gains can be achieved through efficient structuring of the pay package. When pastor and congregation work together cooperatively to find the optimum means of providing compensation, an amazing efficiency occurs. It's often possible to increase the value of the pay package by 10% or more at no additional cost to the church. Let's look at how this occurs.

Cost v. Compensation

There is a critical distinction that must be appreciated between cost to the church and compensation to the pastor. There is a dramatic difference between what the pastor receives and what it costs the church to have a pastor. When working with your personnel committee on compensation issues, make certain this distinction is noted. Separate compensation items into one column, and transfer cost items into another. For instance, a typical church budget might contain the following items:

Pastor's Compensation	Church Cost Items
Salary	Pastors travel
Parsonage utilities	Office expense
Parsonage insurance	Publications and books
Parsonage mortgage	Pastor's continuing education
Pension	Entertaining and gifts
Hospitalization	Vestments

Frequently we encounter church budgets that list all of these items (both columns) under the single heading of Pastoral Support. The implication to the church's members is that the entire total of these items is money in the preacher's pocket. This often results in the erroneous conclusion that the pastor is well compensated when the reality may be quite the contrary. We frequently hear laity remark that their pastor earns more than they do. Upon a challenge from us we discover that lay leaders were making the common error of comparing their take-home pay with the sum of total church expenditures. When this fallacious tactic is practiced, it should be no surprise that the preacher's pay looks pretty good. What's happening, however, is that apples are being compared with oranges. The lay person views his or her pay as an employee and sees only the paycheck, whereas he or she views the pastor's compensation as an employer and sees total cost. Before you even discuss salary, make sure that this cost/compensation differential is understood.

Tax Efficiency is Good Stewardship

In today's world of the bottom line, the number that matters is not how much money you receive. The only meaningful amount is how much you get to keep. It is frequently possible for one parish to provide their pastor with take-home pay substantially higher than a neighboring church's pastor gets—even though each church pays the exact same number of dollars. It's the way the dollars are received that makes all the difference.

Clergy may receive money from the congregation that could have one of three different types of tax liabilities: (1) totally tax-exempt, (2) exempt from income tax but subject to Social

Security (SECA) tax, and (3) subject to both income and Social Security taxes. Here's how.

Professional Expenses—When the church expects the pastor to pay for professional expenses, such as travel, out of the pastor's own pocket, two major errors occur. First is the justice issue of the pastor having to pay what is really a church expense (see above). But a serious tax error also is happening. Although the pastor may be able to deduct professional expenses from taxable income, it's more tax-wise for the church to reimburse the pastor in full for professional expenses. When this occurs true reimbursement is received by the pastor absolutely free of any tax.

Fringe Benefits—Indirect or non-cash compensation provided by the employer for the benefit and convenience of the employee are not subject to any tax. This is a splendid way to increase the value of compensation because the pastor receives the compensation and keeps 100% of the value—no dilution from taxation. Simply calling a benefit a fringe does not render it tax-free. These approved fringe benefits include medical and dental care, optical care, child care, and term life insurance (up to $50,000).

Housing—An important tax benefit for clergy is found in the value of church-provided housing. Section 107 of the Internal Revenue Code provides that compensation for providing a home is not subject to federal income tax. Whether you receive a parsonage or a cash allowance (or both!), there is no income tax liability on this compensation. There is, however, a Social Security tax liability on all housing income. (See chapter 00, on taxes, for a complete examination of this issue.)

Salary—Income received for service as a "minister of the gospel" is subject to federal income tax and self-employment tax (SECA). Since this is the most severe tax burden of all—43.3% for many clergy—it is frequently worth the effort to find ways of providing compensation that are not subject to one or both of these taxes.

Putting the Package Together

Before you negotiate salary, work for a policy on professional expenses. Establishing a true policy of professional expense reimbursement may be the single most important task in developing a compensation package for clergy. It is a justice issue in that an important principle is established: The church should pay for the church's business. Common professional expenses such as travel, books and periodicals, business meals, and entertaining are correctly understood to be the responsibility of the congregation, not the pastor.

The most equitable arrangement is for the church to agree to pay for usual professional expenses necessary for the pastor to carry on the ministry of the church. This, when properly executed, results in no taxable income for the pastor and extra expense for the church for only the actual cost of church business. However, new tax regulations make it more important than ever that these transactions be handled properly. Let's take a look at what is old and what is new in expense reimbursement.

No Change

It has always been necessary to make a clear distinction between an allowance, which has always been taxable income, and true reimbursement, which is not considered income in the first place. An allowance is money that is intended to be distributed to the pastor irrespective of actual expenditures. For example, your church may provide a travel allowance of $3,600 paid out $300 each month. This transaction is, and always has been, just the same tax-wise as if it were salary. The allowance must be included by the church treasurer in preparing the year-end 1099 or W-2 form, and the pastor must declare the full amount as taxable income.

However, reimbursement is a policy, not a price tag. The congregation agrees to pay for professional expenses at a pre-determined rate: cost for purchases, 26 cents/mile for travel, and so forth. As the pastor incurs expenses, a voucher is submitted documenting the expenditure. Upon receipt of voucher, the congregation grants the pastor a check in the amount due. Because this transaction is not interpreted to be compensation (IRC 162 and 274), this amount need not be reported as income.

Recent Changes on Reimbursement Policy

New regulations from IRS substantially tighten the requirements to meet the definitions of reimbursement under IRC 274. Currently, the payor (the congregation in most cases) serves as a sort of auditor. The reimbursement voucher must, to the payor's satisfaction, address the essential elements of true reimbursement:

1. What the expense was (who was entertained, what was purchased).
2. When the expense occurred.
3. Why the expense is business-related (why the item purchased was necessary, why the person was entertained).
4. Where the event/travel occurred.
5. How much was expended (how many miles were traveled).

All five of these elements must be recorded to satisfy the requirements of a reimbursement relationship. When confidentiality issues apply—protecting the name of a parishioner visited at a mental health facility, for example—the pastor may notate that such documentation is available but is withheld at this time. IRS officials have endorsed this important professional issue of confidentiality.

Four additional reimbursement issues to remember in establishing your policy:

1. "Use it or lose it"—any unused balances remaining in the budget must be forfeited. A critical distinction between an allowance and reimbursement is that allowances are always fully disbursed whereas only actual costs are reimbursed.
2. If the congregation is unable to offer additional money on top of salary for professional expenses, an important tax benefit may be achieved by reducing the salary by an agreed upon amount and by establishing a corresponding reimbursement account in the church budget. All of the above policies apply. The pastor receives the money without tax liability as long as payments are made only upon receipt of an expense voucher.
3. Expenses (other than mileage) in excess of $25 must be accompanied by a receipt.
4. Meals and entertainment expenses may be reimbursed at 100% of cost—an important distinction between deductibility and

exclusion. Although such expenses are limited to 80% of cost for income tax deductions, reimbursement may be made in full with no tax liability.

So, you're on the voucher system now. That's good. But at what rate should you be reimbursed? For expenses it should be obvious. You'll be reimbursed for your actual costs. But what about travel? For most clergy, travel is the largest professional expense of all, so it makes good sense to establish this crucial reimbursement correctly.

Payment for professional travel may be at the IRS standard mileage rate (currently 26 cents per mile) or at your level of actual expenses. Many clergy will find their costs substantially in excess of 26 cents per mile. If you elect to be reimbursed at a higher rate, however, you must be able to show how your actual expenses were calculated. Here's an example of how costs might be substantially more than the IRS rate.

"His holiness is never home since they started paying his mileage."

Actual auto lease	-	$3,600
Auto insurance	-	700
Actual fuel expenses	-	900
Repairs & maintenance	-	600
Total expenses		5,800
Less personal use		(1,080)
Net expense		4,720

$4,720 ÷ 15,000 bus. miles = 31.4 cents per mile

Your congregation could give you the equivalent of another $820 tax-free by agreeing to reimburse your actual travel costs rather than 26 cents a mile.

How to Handle Housing

Section 107 of the Internal Revenue Code provides a significant tax break for clergy. Expenses for providing a home are not subject to federal income tax provided that such compensation is established in advance as housing. For pastors who live in a church-provided parsonage, this means that the value of the parsonage need not be included in gross income for income tax purposes. Most clergy know this already.

What is not well-known, however, is that even parsonage-dwellers may receive cash allowances for housing-related items in addition to the parsonage itself. In some parts of the country, the parsonage is furnished, whereas in other areas the parsonage is unfurnished (perhaps with the exception of major appliances). Pastors know that even a furnished parsonage is not without some housing expenses. Decorating items, cleaning supplies, lawn maintenance—these and a variety of other items are customary costs of having a home in addition to furniture.

A tax-wise strategy for all clergy is to receive at least some compensation in the form of a housing/furnishings allowance. If you provide your own home, the amount of this allowance should be sufficient to cover rent/mortgage costs, utilities, taxes (if you own), furnishings, insurance, and maintenance. You may find that 35% or more of total cash compensation could be received in the form of a housing allowance, thereby avoiding thousands of dollars of unnecessary income taxes. If you live in a parsonage, you ought to receive an allowance for furnishings at least sufficient to pay for your annual furnishings acquisitions, renter's insurance premiums, plus any maintenance and utility expenses that are your responsibility. (See pp. 132-33 for a full explanation of this concept.)

Have the church conference or administrative board endorse an annual resolution such as this: "For the year 199x, $6,000 of the Rev. Smith's salary shall be considered an allowance for housing and furnishings under the provisions of Sec. 107 of the Internal Revenue Code." It is important to note that this resolution may save you up to $2,000 of tax while costing the congregation absolutely nothing.

Occasionally a lay person may observe that this tax treatment results in an unfair advantage (loophole) for the preacher. You may wish to point out to such persons that similar benefits are available to lay employees required to live in employer-provided housing for the benefit of the employer—an apartment manager, for example (IRC Sec. 119). In these circumstances, the lay person pays neither income nor Social Security tax on the value of the compensation, whereas the clergy must pay the 15.3% self-employment tax on housing compensation. You also may wish to inquire of your lay persons if they deduct mortgage interest and property taxes. These itemized deductions can be as much as 90% of the cost of home ownership and can offer a tax break for laity nearly equal to the loophole Section 107 provides for clergy.

Fringes and Benefits

As we have noted above, fringe benefits are attractive because they provide a received-benefit equal to 100 cents on every dollar of church cost. Section 105 of the IRS code provides for the exclusion of employer-provided benefits for medical/dental/optical expenses as well as child care and other specified fringes. Although it is possible that some medical expenses could be deducted on Schedule A of your tax return, experience suggests that many parsonage-residing clergy do not have sufficient deductions to itemize. Even those who do exceed the standard deduction ($5,200 for joint filers) may not deduct medical expenses except those exceeding 7½% of adjusted gross income.

A better way is to have the congregation agree to reimburse you fully for any out-of-pocket medical expenses not covered by your health care plan. These might include deductibles, co-pays, exclusions such as check-ups, plus dental and optical costs which might not be covered by insurance at all. Many churches provide additional budgeted amounts for this reimbursement on top of salary. If your church is not willing or able to do so, you still can achieve a substantial benefit by having your salary reduced by a stated amount and by using the corresponding amount to establish a fund from which you can be reimbursed for medical expenses.

Since you can receive these funds only to reimburse yourself for an expense, it is important that your pay not be reduced by more than you're likely to need for medical costs. If you keep careful records, you may know what a typical year's worth of expenses will be. Particularly during the orthodontic years, this benefit can save hundreds of tax dollars—at no additional church expense.

"I GUESS I'LL TAKE MY DATE TO CHURCH...I'M TOO BROKE
TO TAKE HER ANY PLACE ELSE."

Getting an Adequate Salary

As the list below documents, clergy are among the lowest-paid of professionals. There are, doubtless, historic reasons for this phenomenon. However, a heritage of low pay doesn't excuse some of the practices contributing to low clergy salaries. As you negotiate with your committee, try these simple strategies.

How Does Clergy Pay Compare?

In a recent survey by the Bureau of Labor Statistics clergy pay ranked 19th out of 25 major occupational categories. Rankings were based on median pay levels of practicing professionals in the fields surveyed. Results showed what clergy have known all along—clergy and teachers rank last among college-educated professionals.

CLERGY PERSONAL FINANCE

How Does Clergy Pay Compare?

1. Engineers, chemical
2. Lawyers
3. Engineers, industrial
4. Physicians
5. Pharmacists
6. Chemists
7. Computer programmers
8. Public Relations specialists
9. Electricians
10. Accountants
11. Electrical & electronic technicians
12. Police
13. Nurses, registered
14. Teachers, college
15. Librarians
16. Social workers
17. Carpenters
18. Legal assistants
19. Clergy
20. Teachers, secondary school
21. Auto mechanics
22. Typesetters
23. Secretaries
24. File clerks
25. Bank tellers

1. Always begin negotiations with something you know you can win. Start by correcting any defects in working conditions—particularly if the price tag is low. For instance, if you need a sound-proof door on your office for counseling confidentiality, start with that. Who could object to something as pastoral as that? And once the committee has started to say yes, you're off to a great start.

2. Head off any potential complaints by anticipating them and addressing the area of concern. Are people concerned that you're not making pastoral calls? Keep a careful record and provide statistical reports to the committee. At my former parish I discovered that I was making over seven hundred calls

a year. Perhaps you make even more—why hide your light under a bushel?

3. Make sure that inflation adjustments are not understood as raises. Although the amount of dollars involved may have increased substantially, the buying power of the money is exactly the same. All that has happened is inflation adjustment. Following is a chart that documents how inflation during the seventies and eighties more than tripled the amount required to purchase the same value.

Year	Salary	Inflation Rate	
1970	10,000	5.49%	
1971	10,549	3.36	
1972	10,903	3.41	
1973	11,275	8.8	
1974	12,267	12.2	
1975	13,764	7.01	
1976	14,729	4.81	
1977	15,437	6.8	
1978	16,487	9.0	
1979	17,971	13.3	
1980	20,361	12.4	
1981	22,886	8.9	
1982	24,923	3.9	
1983	25,895	3.8	
1984	26,879	3.9	
1985	27,927	3.8	
1986	28,988	1.1	
1987	29,707	4.4	
1988	30,597	4.5	
1989	31,973	4.8	est
1990	33,508		

4. Consider having the church treasurer make your contributions to any pension plan. Although it is true that many (not all) clergy can deduct contributions they make to an Individual Retirement Account (I.R.A.), a better instrument is available for virtually every clergyperson. The tax-deferred annuity, often referred to as a 403(b) plan, offers everything an I.R.A. provides and much more. Although the I.R.A. contribution is a deduction from taxable income, it defers only income tax. You will still be required to pay Social Security tax on the money. The tax-deferred annuity is not a reduction, but

is rather a complete deferral of the income. Since the deferred income is not considered to have been received, you will not pay current income tax (just like the I.R.A.), but you will also permanently avoid the self-employment tax.

On contributions of $2,000, for example, the T.D.A. saves you an additional $306 in taxes. The only prerequisite to qualify for this more favorable tax treatment is that a salary reduction agreement must exist between you and the church, and that the church treasurer must write the check. If you receive the funds and write a personal check, the tax deferral is lost.

Here's how the tax treatment of contributing to an I.R.A. differs from putting the same amount into a tax-deferred annuity (T.D.A.).

I.R.A. Plan		T.D.A. Plan[1]	
Salary	$30,000	Salary	$28,000
I.R.A. contribution	2,000	T.D.A. contribution	2,000
Amount subject to income tax	28,000	Amount subject to income tax	28,000
Amount subject to SECA	30,000	Amount subject to SECA	28,000
Income tax	4,200	Income tax	4,200
SECA	4,590[2]	SECA	4,284[2]
Total Tax	8,790	Total Tax	8,484

Notes: 1. Salary reduced per agreement with church
2. Does not reflect available deduction for half of SECA

5. If your committee offers only what amounts to an inflation adjustment (no real increase), ask what performance goals must be met to deserve a merit increase. Unless the committee is able to tell you how to get a real raise, chances are good that you'll never get one. It is possible that the handwriting is on the wall regarding your future in this congregation. (Note: It may well be that today's congregation

is substantially smaller than it was in 1970. In some situations, the congregation may have to acknowledge that they can no longer afford a ministry comparable to the level they enjoyed twenty years ago.)

Good stewardship and efficiency demand that we strive to structure the pay package to provide maximum benefit to the clergy at minimum cost to the congregation. Although these may seem like conflicting goals, with a little effort and education, you can increase your after-tax compensation substantially with minimal extra cost to the church.

Compensation Planning When You Move

You've unpacked, used your going-away present to buy new curtains for the parsonage, and memorized the church's pictorial directory. Now there's one more important task to do before you settle into that new appointment. Before you do anything else, get your new congregation to establish your compensation package correctly.

That's right. The very same pay package your previous congregation worked so hard on last fall is no longer in place; you will need a new agreement with your current church. Here are three significant agreements that can save you hundreds of dollars but will not even exist until the new congregation acts upon them:

1. Housing/Furnishings Allowance—Establishing this allowance in advance of expenditures can exclude the entire amount from income tax. Remember the three requirements from Section 107: Allowance established in advance cannot exceed fair rental value and must be spent on allowable furnishings items.
2. Professional Expense Reimbursement—You shouldn't have to pay for the congregation's expenses such as periodicals, entertaining, and such. Establish the principle that the church will pay all these expenses, even if your salary must be reduced accordingly the first year.
3. Tax-Deferred Annuity—These salary reduction plans of deferring compensation are the most tax-efficient means of saving for retirement. Nevertheless, you'll need a new formal agreement with the new congregation. Remember that the maximum you can defer is 25% of cash salary (housing is not a part of this base since it is not subject to income tax). It is important to remember that your denominational pension contributions are considered part of the 25%.

Properly structuring the compensation package can increase the value of your pay by 10% or more, but a new plan is necessary each time you move. Don't wait until next year to do what will help today.

Social Security Allowances—a Justice Issue

Congregations that employ clergy enjoy a tremendous tax loophole—they pay no Social Security payroll tax on the minister's pay. Unlike salaries for the secretary, the organist, or the custodian, there is no FICA liability on clergy income. This saves the church hundreds of dollars each year in payroll taxes.

Recognizing that it is inequitable to expect the pastor to pay all the Social Security tax bill when all others share the burden between employee and employer, many thoughtful congregations are establishing allowances for the pastor to help pay some of this cost. Some churches give the pastor the amount that would be the employer's share of the Social Security tax (7.65% currently). Other churches pay the difference between the employee share and self-employment rate (after taxes—5.5% in the 28% bracket, 6.5% in the 15% bracket). In either case the pastor would receive additional taxable compensation subject to both income and self-employment tax. Nevertheless, it's extra money and an appropriate action for a church to take.

We've suggested this strategy to dozens of congregations, and no lay leaders have objected to it. However, you'll have to take the initiative to rectify this justice issue.

As an example of a T.D.A. agreement between an employee minister and an employer church, look at the forms on pages 72-74 used by The United Methodist Church.

Planning for Retirement

For most clergy, retirement presents the greatest financial planning challenge of all. With dramatic changes in income, housing, and expenses, everything seems up for grabs. But don't panic. A little planning (and the discipline to stay with the plan!) should be sufficient to get you into a secure retirement. Because we have addressed the critical issue of providing for your retirement home in chapter 9, here we will explore ways to meet your retirement income goals.

An essential step in your retirement planning is the calculation of your future retirement benefits. Although many clergy do have a fair idea of their likely pension benefits, few understand the relationship between pension funds, Social Security, and individual investments. What will you require to live on, without unusual sacrifice, when you retire? Where will those funds come from? Let's take a look at determining answers to these questions.

1. Perhaps the first step in the process is to ascertain your credits for Social Security and pension contributions. Request a statement showing your service from your denominational pension office. If you have a "defined benefit" pension plan, you need only to multiply the annuity rate times your years of approved service. Defined contribution plans will require you (or your advisor) to do a present-value analysis of the likely future amount.

2. Request a record of your Social Security earnings from the

FACTS ABOUT YOUR SOCIAL SECURITY

THE FACTS
YOU GAVE US

Your Name...
Your Social Security Number.....................
Your Date of Birth...................................January 8, 1945
1987 Earnings...$25,800
1988 Earnings...$26,000
Your Estimated Future Average Yearly Earnings
....$26,000
The Age You Plan To Retire.......................................62

We used these facts and the information already on our records to prepare this statement for you. When we estimated your benefits, we included any 1987 and 1988 earnings you told us about. We also included any future estimated earnings up to the age you told us you plan to retire.

If you did not estimate your future earnings, we did not project any future earnings for you.

YOUR
SOCIAL
SECURITY
EARNINGS

The chart below shows the earnings on your Social Security record. It also estimates the amount of Social Security taxes you paid each year to finance benefits under Social Security and Medicare. We show earnings only up to the maximum amount of yearly earnings covered by Social Security. These maximum amounts are also shown on the chart. The chart may not include some or all of your earnings from last year because they may not have been posted to your record yet.

Years	Maximum Yearly Earnings Subject to S.S. Tax	Your S.S. Taxed Earnings	Estimated S.S. Taxes You Paid	Years	Maximum Yearly Earnings Subject to S.S. Tax	Your S.S. Taxed Earnings	Estimated S.S. Taxes You Paid
1937-1950	$3,000	$ 0	$ 0	1970	$ 7,800	$ 3,309	$ 158
1951	3,600	0	0	1971	7,800	3,753	281
1952	3,600	0	0	1972	9,000	4,379	328
1953	3,600	0	0	1973	10,800	6,210	496
1954	3,600	0	0	1974	13,200	7,505	599
1955	4,200	0	0	1975	14,100	10,610	810
1956	4,200	0	0	1976	15,300	12,264	968
1957	4,200	0	0	1977	16,500	12,974	1,024
1958	4,200	0	0	1978	17,700	14,591	1,181
1959	4,800	0	0	1979	22,900	16,490	1,335
1960	4,800	0	0	1980	25,900	17,378	1,407
1961	4,800	0	0	1981	29,700	17,485	1,626
1962	4,800	195	6	1982	32,400	19,391	1,813
1963	4,800	1,024	37	1983	35,700	18,163	1,698
1964	4,800	0	0	1984	37,800	19,754	2,232
1965	4,800	1,426	51	1985	39,600	20,506	2,419
1966	6,600	3,534	148	1986	42,000	25,168	3,095
1967	6,600	4,472	196	1987	43,800	25,811	3,174
1968	7,800	5,030	221	1988	45,000	0	0
1969	7,800	5,019	240	1989		0	0

YOUR
SOCIAL
SECURITY
CREDITS

To qualify for benefits, you need credit for a certain amount of work covered by Social Security. The number of credits you need will vary with the type of benefit. Under current law, you do not need more than 40 credits to be fully insured for any benefit. (See "How You Earn Social Security Credits" on the reverse side.)

Our review of your earnings, including any 1987 and 1988 earnings you told us about, shows that you now have at least 40 Social Security credits.

ESTIMATED BENEFITS

RETIREMENT   You must have 40 Social Security credits to be fully insured for retirement benefits. Assuming that you meet all the requirements, here are estimates of your retirement benefits based on your past and any projected earnings. The estimates are in today's dollars, but adjusted to account for average wage growth in the national economy.

If you retire at 62, your monthly benefit in today's dollars will be about.. $ 725

The earliest age at which you can receive an unreduced retirement benefit is 66 years of age. We call this your full retirement age. If you work until that age and then retire, your monthly benefit in today's dollars will be about.. $ 980

If you continue to work and wait until you are 70 to receive benefits, your monthly benefit in today's dollars will be about............................$1,305

SURVIVORS   If you have a family, you must have 21 Social Security credits for certain family members to receive benefits if you were to die this year. They may also qualify if you earn 6 credits in the 3 years before your death. The number of credits a person needs to be insured for survivors benefits increases each year until age 62, up to a maximum of 40 credits. Here is an estimate of the benefits your family could receive if you had enough credits to be insured, they qualified for benefits, and you died this year:

Your child could receive a monthly benefit of about.................. $ 585

If your child and your surviving spouse who is caring for your child both qualify, they could each receive a monthly benefit of about.......$ 585

When your surviving spouse reaches full retirement age, he or she could receive a monthly benefit of about..$ 780

The total amount that we could pay your family each month is about $1,365

We may also be able to pay your surviving spouse or children a one-time death benefit of... $ 255

DISABILITY   Right now, you must have 21 Social Security credits to be insured for disability benefits. And, 20 of these credits had to be earned in the 10 year period immediately before you became disabled. If you are blind or received disability benefits in the past, you may need fewer credits. The number of credits a person needs to be insured for disability benefits increases each year until age 62, up to a maximum of 40 credits.

If you were disabled, had enough credits, and met the other requirements for disability benefits, here is an estimate of the benefits you could receive right now:

Your monthly benefit would be about.. $ 750

You and your eligible family members could receive up to a monthly total of about...$1,125

IF YOU HAVE QUESTIONS   If you have any questions about this statement, please read the information on the reverse side. If you still have questions, please call 1-800-937-7005.

Social Security Administration. A postcard requesting this information is available at all Social Security offices. Experts recommend receiving this information every three years.

Here's an example of what you will receive from the Social Security Administration when you request your earnings record. Check the amounts under the earnings column. Do any of the years seem out of line to you? If an amount looks too high or too low, check your tax records. Although rare, it is possible for your account to be credited with someone else's earnings record. More likely, though, your records will be accurate. Now, note the estimated benefits statement. One of the good things about this is that benefits are expressed in

"Probably a former clergyman trying to live on faith, hope and social security."

terms of today's buying power. In our example, full benefits are estimated to be $980 per month. The actual benefits (approximately twenty years from now) will be close to $2,600 per month, but this figure is virtually meaningless unless we know what $2,600 will be worth then. Expressing the benefit in today's dollars ($980/month) is a more realistic way of presenting this information.

3. Compute the percentage of current income your benefits will represent. This is called the "replacement ratio." You may compute the replacement ratio formula by dividing benefits by current income.

For example, a pastor retiring this year at age sixty-five is receiving $31,000 of current income (salary and housing). Her Social Security benefits are $698 per month—$8,376 per year. This pastor's replacement ratio for Social Security benefits is 27% (8,376 ÷ $31,000 = .27).

In general, the higher your pay, the lower the replacement ratio represented by Social Security benefits will be. The average is 41%.

4. Add to your Social Security benefit the replacement ratio provided by your pension plan. United Methodists, for instance, may plan on about 1% of an average salary for each year of service. (Note, however, that your salary near retirement is likely to be above average, so the replacement ratio will be proportionately smaller.) Today 25% is a good pension plan ratio.

To the 27% Social Security ratio, our example pastor adds the 25% provided by pension and discovers that these two sources will produce 52% of her current income.

5. Figure what you will require to live in retirement. Most clergy will require 70 to 80% of pre-retirement income, perhaps more if you have not provided for retirement housing.

6. Structure your savings/investment strategy to produce retirement income sufficient to meet your total replacement ratio requirement. Assuming our pastor needs 70%, she will require investment income producing the 18% not provided by pension and Social Security benefits.

Using conservative assumptions about return (and you should), you will need about $20,000 to generate each $100 of monthly income. Anything less than this earns less than 6% (our conservative assumption) and will require you to invade your capital.

Because our example pastor must replace more than $250 a month from investments to meet her 70% goal, she will require more than $50,000 in investments. Here an annuity may be a smart alternative for a pastor who does not wish to risk market upheaval or depletion of the investment for whatever reason. The same $250 per month could be provided by a single life annuity for about $30,000 at age sixty-five. You will have nothing left to leave heirs with an annuity, but you cannot outlive an annuity, either.

You may accomplish the same purpose as an annuity simply by taking an amount from your savings each year which may equal the annuity you would have purchased. For instance, if you would invest your $30,000 nest egg at 8%, you would withdraw $250 each month for twenty years before the principal was depleted. If you could earn more than 8%, or if you died before the end of the twenty years, the money would be left for your heirs.

By starting with a single $10,000 investment, which earns 7% interest annually, the following chart shows how you can create your own annuity through a combination of principal and interest withdrawals each month. Note: It may be helpful to know that the life expectancy of a sixty-five-year-old today is nearly twenty years!

The following amounts can be withdrawn monthly for the stated number of years until the $10,000 principal is depleted.

MONTHLY WITHDRAWAL

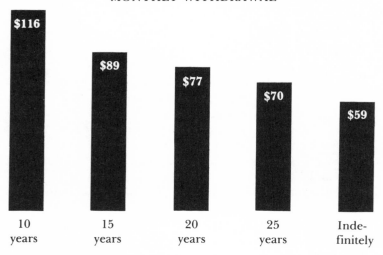

This decision, like most basic monetary decisions, will be largely determined by our comfort level with risk and uncertainty. If you cannot abide the prospect that interest rates fall as well as rise, of if you cannot trust yourself to keep hands off your capital, an annuity might be the best option.

How Social Security Fits Into Retirement Planning

Although the vast majority of clergy will be eligible to receive retirement income from Social Security, a much smaller percentage of clergy really understand what those benefits will be or how the benefits are calculated. We regularly encounter clergy late in their careers who are making extra payments of Social Security tax in the mistaken belief that this will increase future benefits.

In spite of what you may have heard in the past, retirement benefits for Social Security are not based on your last three or five years of earnings. For clergy retiring today or in the future, benefits are computed using a system known as indexing. Starting with 1950, each year's earnings (and the taxes paid on them) are assigned a value derived by multiplying the earnings by an inflation-adjusted number for that year. What this means is that any individual year's earnings are blended with those of your entire career, making it impossible to make a significant impact on retirement benefits in a few years.

What is also frequently misunderstood about Social Security benefits is that they are only indirectly related to income earned. That is to say that benefits do not increase proportionately as earnings (and taxes) rise. Here's a chart illustrating how benefits are related to earnings levels and the resultant Social Security taxes. Each exhibit assumes full benefits for a person currently eight years from eligibility (now age fifty-seven).

Current Income	S.S. Tax	Future Benefits
$16,000	$2,080	$6,624 Annually
23,000	2,990	8,460 Annually
31,000	4,030	9,036 Annually
40,000	5,200	9,468 Annually

Notice how benefits increase much slower than taxes. For example, from $23,000 to $31,000 of income, taxes increase by 35% whereas benefits rise only 7%. From $31,000 to $40,000, taxes jump 29% whereas benefits are increased only 5%.

But you don't have to wait until age sixty-five. (Note: The "normal retirement age" is being increased from sixty-five years to sixty-seven years. It works like this: If you were born between 1943 and 1954, your normal retirement age is sixty-six. If you were born between 1955 and 1959, your normal retirement age is your sixty-sixth birthday plus two months for every year beyond 1954 until your birth year. If you were born in 1960 or later, your normal retirement age is sixty-seven.) You may elect to receive reduced benefits as early as three years before you're due for full benefits. The price you pay for this early retirement option is a reduction of 6⅔% for each year you retire early. Should you retire at the earliest age (currently age sixty-two), your benefits would be reduced by 20%. I am frequently asked if this is a good deal. Assuming you can afford to retire at age sixty-two, the numbers usually demonstrate the advantage of "take the money and run." Here's why.

If you decide to wait until your normal retirement age, you'll receive higher benefits. However, you'll also give up thousands of dollars in benefits you would have received had you retired early. Assume that in 1992 you could retire early with reduced benefits equal to 80% of full benefits—full benefits would have been $700/month ($8,400 annually), so reduced benefits will be $560/month ($6,720 annually). During the three years from retirement eligibility until normal retirement, you will forego more than $20,000 in benefits you might have received. To determine if waiting three more years for benefits is worth it, you will need to weigh the value of future benefits compared to lost early benefits.

Year	Social Security Benefits (early retirement)	Social Security Benefits (regular retirement)
1992	$ 6,720	$ 0
1993	6,989	0
1994	7,268	0
1995	7,559	9,449

1996	$ 7,861	$ 9,827
1997	8,176	10,220
1998	8,503	10,629
1999	8,843	11,054
2000	9,197	11,496
2001	9,565	11,956
2002	9,947	12,434
2003	10,345	12,932
2004	10,759	13,449
2005	11,189	13,987
2006	11,636	14,546
Total benefits received	$134,557	$141,979

You will note that total benefits received do not catch up with the early retirement option until age seventy-seven, which is twelve years after full retirement benefits begin. This comparison does not even attempt to analyze the present value of receiving a substantial amount early. A true evaluation of the two columns would weigh the value so heavily in favor of early payments that it would take at least fifteen years of full benefits to catch up.

If you are married, your spouse will be eligible for Social Security benefits as well. Spouses with work histories of their own may be wise to elect benefits based on their own earnings, or, if career earnings are low, the spouse may choose spousal benefits equal to 50% of your benefit. Ask Social Security to compute estimates both ways to help make the decision.

How Taxes Influence Retirement Income

One of the good things about Social Security benefits is that they may be received tax free. I say *may* be received tax free because the Tax Reform Act of 1986 now subjects up to half the Social Security payments of certain high income taxpayers to federal income tax. (Currently, married taxpayers filing jointly pay income tax on Social Security when total income—including tax-exempt municipal bonds interest and 50% of Social Security income—exceeds $32,000.)

What this tax-free treatment of Social Security means is that the value of your Social Security income is substantially higher than it might otherwise appear. For example, when deciding whether your projected retirement income will be enough to replace your current salary (see replacement ratios, pp. 120-21), consider that you probably keep only $.57 or less of much of the salary you receive. How? Subtract $.28 for federal income tax and take away an additional $.15 for self-employment tax, plus reductions for any applicable state/local income taxes. The most you can expect to have left is $.57. If your salary today is $2,500 per month and your Social Security benefits are $750 per month, recognize that your after-tax salary income might really be only $1,425 ($2,500 × .57 = $1,425). Note that the $750 Social Security benefits appears to represent only 30% of current salary; however, compared to the take-home portion of your pay ($1,425), your benefit really replaces more than half (52.6%) of your pay.

Your pension income may have important tax-favored treatment as well. Although most pension income is taxable, an important tax benefit is available for clergy who know how to use it. Section 107 of the tax code allows clergy, including retired clergy, to exclude from taxable income the amount received to provide a home. This means that as long as your pension is designated as an allowance for housing, up to 100% of pension income may escape tax. An important caveat regarding this tax treatment is that the funds must actually be used for housing expenditures. In many cases this will not be difficult. Here's how it might work.

Annual pension income	$9,000	$750/month
Less housing expenses		
	5,000	mortgage payments
	2,000	utilities
	1,500	property taxes
	700	furnishings
Total housing expenses	$9,200	
Taxable pension income	$ 0	

See chapter 14 for a more detailed account of clergy housing issues related to Section 107. It is also important to note in your retirement planning that this income exclusion does not extend to the surviving spouse of a clergyperson. Upon your death your spouse may have to pay tax on all the pension benefit received, subject to other variables such as deductions and personal exemptions.

What the tax treatment of Social Security and pension income means to you is that less may be more. Remember the example we shared on the preceding page. The pastor currently earning $2,500 per month may discover that the sum of Social Security and pension benefits (tax free) may be more than the net of current salary after taxes. Add $750 per month Social Security to $750 pension, and it equals $1,500 each month compared to $1,425 net salary. The important variable here is that the working pastor likely lives in a church-provided parsonage, whereas the retiree must provide (and pay for) all housing expenses.

How Much Is Your Social Security Worth?

It's popular these days to "bad mouth" Social Security. Many clergy are absolutely convinced that they could achieve a better return on Social Security tax money by investing the funds elsewhere. We won't try to convince you that you're wrong or right, but do recognize one crucial fact about Social Security benefits: Social Security is an insurance plan, not just a retirement income investment.

Let's assume that you are a young clergyperson age thirty-five with a spouse the same age and two children. Do you realize that you already have over a million dollars of Social Security insurance? It's true. Here's what you already have.

Survivor's insurance	$ 454,480
Disability insurance	$ 386,160
Retirement income	$ 218,880
Total	$1,059,520

Before you try to compare your "bang for the buck" from Social Security, at least remember what is included in the package.

14

Tax Planning

What's the biggest expenditure most persons experience? No, it's not food or housing or automobile expenses. The biggest expense in your life is taxes. Knowing how to avoid unnecessary tax costs can be the best strategy for discovering funds to contribute toward your saving/investment goals.

Because a variety of good tax preparation material is available (we particularly recommend the annual *Abingdon Clergy Income Tax Guide*), we will not attempt to duplicate such guides here. We will, instead, point out several critical issues to help you plan your tax life for maximum efficiency and compliance with current tax codes and treasury regulations.

Tax rules are dynamic and continually changing. It's always a good idea to get tax information from the most up-to-date source. Material included in this chapter is accurate as of its publishing date.

In this chapter you will find help in understanding your tax status (employee or independent contractor), clergy housing issues, handling professional expenses, calculating self-employment taxes, and additional aids in the process of tax planning.

How to Declare Your Income

For years the battle has raged: Are clergy self-employed independent contractors or are they common law employees?

As far as the IRS is concerned, the matter is simple: Clergy who receive salaries from a local congregation are employees for income tax purposes while retaining self-employment status for Social Security. The apparent inconsistency is not denied by the IRS, which instead points out that the self-employment status for Social Security merely relates to the Social Security tax rates, not employment status generally. Clergy who wish to contend they are self-employed will need to establish this on separate grounds.

Of immediate concern to both pastor and congregation is which IRS form is appropriate to document church income: W-2 for common law employee clergy or 1099-MISC for self-employed clergy. Frequently, church treasurers will issue a W-2 form to the pastor along with the rest of the church staff in the mistaken view that IRS Revenue Ruling 80-110 requires a W-2. Recent tax court cases have established that, for example, United Methodist clergy may be considered self-employed if the facts of the case substantiate it.

In *Cosby v. Commissioner of Internal Revenue,* the court found that a United Methodist pastor was correct in declaring income and deducting professional expenses on Schedule C. *Cosby,* decided in 1987, dealt with a 1980 tax return, but recently the IRS acceded on a similar set of facts on a 1982 return (*Cooper v. Commissioner of Internal Revenue*). It is important to note that the judge in *Cosby* cited the issuance of the appropriate income statement (W-2 or 1099) as a significant documentation of "the relationship the parties believe they created." If the treasurer issues a W-2, this mitigates against a claim of self-employment. Although the W-2 does not prohibit use of Schedule C, it would probably be best to request the reissuance of a 1099-MISC.

Having considered all of these issues, I still believe that clergy in many denominations have an excellent chance to establish their relationship as independent contractors. Section 31.3401(c)-1(b) describes the employer/employee relationship in ways that suggest that United Methodists, for example, are more likely self-employed rather than common law employees.

If the treasurer resists this position, refer him or her to Section 31.3401(c)-1(b), which states:

Generally the relationship of employer and employee exists when the person for whom services are performed has the right to control and direct the individual who performs the services, not only as to the results to be accomplished by the work, but also as to the details and means by which that result is accomplished. That is, an employee is subject to the will of and control of the employer not only as to what shall be done but how it shall be done. In this connection, it is not necessary that the employer actually direct or control the manner in which services are performed; it is sufficient that he has the right to do so. The right to discharge is also an important factor indicating that the person possessing that right is an employer. Other factors characteristic of an employer, but not necessarily present in every case, are the furnishing of tools and the furnishing of a place to work to the individual who performs the service. In general, if an individual is subject to the control or direction of another merely as to the result to be accomplished by the work and not as to the means and methods of accomplishing the result, he is not an employee.

Also, appropriate would be an analysis of Revenue Ruling 87-41, which spells out twenty issues to be examined in determining employment status. In my judgment, United Methodist clergy fall into the independent contractor category in at least ten of the twenty tests, and in the employee column only seven times, with the remainder ambiguous.

What this suggests is that United Methodist clergy income should be declared on Schedule C. *Note:* Even non-Methodist clergy who do not claim self-employment will need to use Schedule C to declare honoraria (see the section Honoraria Are Taxable Income in this chapter).

If you are not United Methodist, or if you conclude that your relationship with the congregation more closely approximates that of an employee, declare your income on line seven of your 1040.

Note: Copies of *Cosby v. Commissioner* and interpretations of Revenue Ruling 87-41 are available from Clergy Financial Services (P.O. Box 6007, Grand Rapids, MI 49516). Send a stamped self-addressed envelope and $1.00 for each copy you request.

Honoraria Are Taxable Income

Most pastors regularly receive honoraria for officiating at weddings and funerals. Although some clergy presumably consider such honoraria as gifts, the IRS is emphatic that these are fees, professional compensation, and fully liable for tax purposes. Even if you turn these honoraria over to the local congregation, you must report them as income. You may, of course, deduct any honoraria you do turn over to the church.

Making Sense of Clergy Housing

Perhaps the most misunderstood concept in clergy taxation is the tax treatment of housing. The tax code provides a valuable tax shelter for all ministers of the gospel who learn how to utilize this powerful advantage.

Section 107 of the Internal Revenue Code of 1986 provides that "in the case of a minister of the gospel, gross income does not include—(1). the rental value of a home furnished as part of compensation; or (2). the rental allowance paid as part of compensation, to the extent used to provide a home."

In recent years the IRS has taken a rather broad view of what qualifies for the clergy housing exclusion and a rather narrow view of how this exclusion must be applied. What this implies is that care must be taken to establish the allowance for housing or furnishings properly but that, once established, the allowance may be used for a wide variety of home furnishing items including but not limited to:

furniture—including appliances
decorating—draperies, rugs and carpet, painting
utilities—garbage removal, cable T.V. (including movie channels), phone (including long distance)
miscellaneous—renter's insurance, snow removal, lawn care, pool maintenance, lawn mower repair and gas

It is absolutely vital that this allowance for furnishings/ housing be properly established. Here's how.

1. Allowance must be established in advance. It is not possible to create this relationship retroactively. You will need

a resolution declaring a portion of your compensation to be an allowance for housing/furnishing.

2. To qualify for the housing exclusion, the funds must actually be expended for the intended purpose. This means that simply calling your salary a housing allowance will not, by that action, exclude it from tax. You must keep careful records of all housing/furnishing expenditures. If you fail to spend all of your allowance, the unused balance must be declared as additional taxable income. Conversely, expenditures in excess of the pre-established amount do not qualify for the exclusion. *Note:* in spite of what some tax advisors are advocating, the expenditure requirement seemingly would invalidate attempts to take a rental allowance for existing furniture. This strategy attempts to shelter income with a type of depreciation for furniture purchased in prior years. While seemingly convincing arguments may be presented for the alleged equity of this arrangement, I believe that the strategy fails the expense test since no expenditure is made.

3. Excluded amounts may not exceed the fair rental value of the property. For furnishings this suggests that the maximum amount excludable in a given year would be the fair rental value of all your furniture.

It is important to recognize that this amount is an exclusion, not a deduction. This means that the allowance for housing/furnishings should *not* be included on a church-provided W-2 form or a 1099.

In spite of the fact that housing, received in a parsonage or through an allowance, is excluded from income for income tax purposes, it is subject to Social Security tax. This means that the amount of income you declare on Form 1040 SE will be higher than the amount declared on the front of 1040 (line 7or 13). See the section Calculating Your Self-Employment Tax in this chapter.

Professional Expense Deductions to Remember

Check your records to determine if you have any of these commonly incurred clergy expenses.

Auto expenses—Were you reimbursed less than 26 cents per mile? The balance for each mile is deductible. Did you buy a car last year? You may deduct the sales tax on Schedule C if you keep track of actual car expenses (if you file as self-employed). Did they exceed your allowance? Balance is deductible.

Charged purchases—The expense is deductible if you use a bank card like Visa or Mastercard, even if you pay next year. However, if you charged the item on a store charge account (for example, the office supply store invoices you) the deduction occurs when the payment is paid.

Entertainment—When you have church members over for a meal or even just coffee you are incurring a deductible entertainment expense. You will need to supply receipts for expenses over $25; otherwise an expense record should suffice. For example, you invite two couples over after administrative council meetings for pie and coffee. You need not document costs of the ingredients for the pie, coffee, sugar, and cream. Instead, take a reasonable deduction of $2.00 per person (including yourself and spouse) for the dessert and beverage. Note: Entertainment deductions are now limited to 80% of costs.

Periodicals—Tax rulings have substantiated that clergy may deduct any periodicals that improve their skills. This includes the daily newspaper, general interest magazines such as *Newsweek*, and any clergy journals to which you subscribe.

Office supplies—While it is better for the church to pay for office expenses, your costs are deductible.

Depreciation—Be sure to depreciate office furniture and machinery you own unless you have previously expensed it. I prefer expensing durable goods instead of depreciating.

Professional clothing—Pulpit robes, stoles, including cleaning expenses. You may not deduct expenses for street clothes that are suitable for professional use. No, you can't deduct your black suit even if you wear it only for funerals.

Dues and memberships—Your dues to local ministerial alliances, church professional groups, and associations may be deducted on Schedule C (if applicable) or Schedule A-Misc.

Gifts—Up to $25 per person. Did you take your secretary out to lunch for Secretary's Week? Christmas gifts to staff, birthday, anniversary, and Christmas cards to parishioners (including postage) are deductible.

Insurance—Do you have to insure your books and office equipment separately from the church's policy even though your office is in the church? Most clergy do. If you do, that portion of your renter's furnishing policy is deductible as a professional expense.

Education expenses—In general, you may deduct expenses for maintaining or improving skills required in your current profession. You may not deduct expenses for qualifying for a new profession. Thus you could take courses in social work, for example, on the grounds that they improve your pastoral counseling skills. However, if you continued these courses until you receive a master of social work degree, the expenses would not be deductible since it qualifies you for a new career—even if you never practice social work.

Calculating Your Self-Employment Tax

One of the crucial distinctions for clergy taxation is the different basis for self-employment tax and income tax. The value of housing received by clergy, whether in the form of a parsonage or a cash allowance, is not subject to income tax but is subject to self-employment tax (Social Security). This means that the base for calculating income tax liability will be quite different from your self-employment tax base.

Begin with your net business income—generally your cash salary less deductible professional expenses. This is the base for computing income tax liability. To this you must add (1) the actual amount of utilities furnished by the church, (2) any tax-exempt allowances for furnishings, and (3) the fair-rental value of the parsonage unfurnished. A traditional rule suggested utilizing 1% of the value of the parsonage per month as an indicator of fair rental value. Today, however, rents are often lower than 1% of market value so you may wish to consult a realtor for a more accurate evaluation.

Tax Avoidance v. Tax Evasion

When clergy set out to prepare their income tax returns they often approach the matter with a certain ambivalence. On the one hand economics dictates that taxes be kept as low as possible; on the other hand is a mystique suggesting that tax reduction methods are somehow unethical. Let me be absolutely clear that I don't mean to suggest that taxes be evaded, illegally dodged. Tax evasion is, and always will be, a crime for clergy and laity alike. Tax avoidance, however, is not only good planning, but sound stewardship as well.

Judge Learned Hand of the U.S. Supreme Court observed long ago: "Over and over again the courts have said that there is nothing sinister in so arranging one's affairs as to keep taxes as low as possible. Everybody does so, rich or poor, and all do right, for nobody owes a public duty to pay more than the law demands. Taxes are enforced extractions, not voluntary contributions." This endorsement of tax planning is clearly about tax avoidance. Yet it also suggests that we seriously examine our tax returns to see if we are, in fact, to take advantage of the tax-saving strategies available to all of us.

Tax Strategies for Better Record-keeping

Once you've completed the ordeal of tax preparation, don't forget the resolution you muttered half-way through the task, "I've got to start keeping better records!" It's not too late to clean up your act for 199x. Here are three easy strategies to make record-keeping less taxing.

Strategy #1—Get a shoe box (or a big envelope or some other receptacle). Half of the task of record-keeping is having a place to keep the records in the first place. While those of you who are organized probably already have elaborate filing systems for receipts and records, the rest of us can start with an ordinary shoe box. Put all receipts and canceled checks in the shoe box. Then, when tax preparation time rolls around, you'll at least know where to go to retrieve vital records.

Strategy #2—Use your bank card. One of the free services of credit cards is the forced record-keeping they provide. Each month you will receive an itemized statement of all expenses along with the bill). As long as you pay the balance in full each month there is no charge for this service.

An alternative to the credit card is a travel and leisure card like American Express or Diners Club. These cards charge an annual membership fee and require you to pay balances in full each month, but they also provide year-end statements that organize all your expenses and categorize them.

Strategy #3—Record expenses in your "daily suggester" or other calendar. As a general rule, only expenses over $25 require a receipt, so smaller items (such as a tank of gas) only require a "contemporaneous record." While a wide variety of clergy expense books are available, you may find that all you need is a place to get down (1) what you spent, (2) what it was for, and (3) why you bought it.

Keeping accurate records may seem like a hassle but it can make a world of difference. One pastor began to keep careful records of small items like greeting cards, postage, and business meals and discovered they totaled over $1,100 in one year. Having the records enabled him to deduct it all and save over $400 in unnecessary taxes.

Deducting Gifts to the Church

One of the things I like most about the clergy is that they seldom need to be talked into giving to the church. One of the things I like least about the clergy is the lengths they sometimes go to garner a tax deduction for charitable giving.

As most of us know all too well, 1986 was the first and last year that non-itemizers could take a full deduction for charitable gifts on top of the standard deduction. Now only those who itemize on Schedule A may deduct charitable donations at all. This has not stopped creative pastors who have embraced any number of strategies in an effort to have the best of a higher standard deduction plus a 100% write-off of church pledges.

The most common ploy used to this end is to have the congregation reduce the pastor's salary by the amount the clergyperson intended to give anyway. While this strategy, if carried to its logical conclusion, would apparently accomplish its goal of reduced taxes (both income and Social Security), it has several difficulties. Merely to have the church keep or withhold the money does not avoid what accountants call constructive receipt. Merely to have the right to the money is to receive it for tax purposes. The congregation must completely eliminate any reference to the proposed amount to be contributed by the pastor. The budget may show only the amount the pastor will receive, not the salary plus tithe.

Where this salary reduction is complete—the same figure reported to the IRS, congregation and annual conference—I suspect that no laws are broken. There are, however, several other practical considerations.

The lower pay results in reductions in both income taxes and Social Security taxes. This will reduce future Social Security benefits somewhat. Pension payments and benefits may be reduced, as well. Finally, under-reporting income results in erroneous information about your current level of compensation. You may discover that the price you pay for avoiding a few hundred dollars of tax is a permanent reduction of your market value as you report a less than representative level of compensation. Don't be surprised if your next appointment, while presumed to be a promotion, is actually a pay cut. Presumably, the only remedy to this syndrome is to admit that you've been defrauding the IRS by under-reporting your income all these years.

We encounter less frequently, but with regularity, a second proposal to deduct church contributions through use of Schedule C. This strategy, say so-called clergy tax experts, involves deducting church contributions on Schedule C as a return. The logic behind the maneuver is that what comes from the church and is given back to the church is a return, right? Wrong! A return on Schedule C is any item that was brought back after a sale. If the item had not been returned the customer would have been contractually obliged to pay for the item. I have heard attempts to buttress this ploy by having the congregation resolve that the pastor must tithe or give an amount equal to the pastor's contribution. It is doubtful, however, whether such resolutions would hold up since employers are not normally allowed to require charitable gifts as a condition of employment.

It is no doubt true that one of the unfortunate side effects of tax reform is the elimination of the charitable deduction for most clergy (those who don't itemize on Schedule A). Nevertheless, we cannot endorse either of the attempts described above to have the best of a big standard deduction and full deductibility of church giving.

One strategy for deducting charitable contributions that we do recommend is "doubling up." Under this strategy, charitable gifts to churches and other charities are pre-paid in December of the preceding year. These contributions, along with those of the current year, presumably would make it more likely that pastors would have enough deductions to exceed the standard deduction. This doubling up results in the standard deduction being claimed every other year with itemization in intervening years. Check it out to determine if doubling up would enable you to obtain a charitable deduction for contributions.

Cosby v. Commissioner Offers New Guidelines
UMC—1, IRS—0

United Methodist and other episcopally appointed clergy shared in a major tax court victory in the case of *Cosby v. Commissioner of Internal Revenue.* In 1987 the tax court ruled that James Cosby, a United Methodist pastor appointed to serve a two-point charge in the Northwest Texas Annual Conference, may deduct professional expenses on Schedule C.

It is important to note the grounds upon which Judge Couvillion based his decision. First, the judge found insufficient evidence of control exercised by The United Methodist Church to support the IRS position that Cosby was an employee. The court noted that provisions in *The Book of Discipline* for removal of United Methodist ministers "do not at all approximate the type of day-to-day supervision and control which is characteristic of an employer-employee relationship."

Second, the court made note of the "substantial capital investment in his ministry: He attended Asbury Theological Seminary in Wilmore, Kentucky, and earned a Master of Divinity degree from that institution." The clergyman, through this "substantial capital investment," provided his own tools of the trade.

Similarly the court rejected the IRS position that services provided by a minister did not require any special skill. Clergy everywhere were affirmed by Judge Couvillion's declaration: "While it may be said that members of the clergy do not possess a skill in the sense that a carpenter builds or a musician plays, we are loath to hold that there is no skill involved in the profession to which members of the clergy find themselves

'Called.' On the contrary, successful ministering, like most professions the goal of which is to positively touch human lives, requires a great deal of skill and compassion. We will not hold otherwise."

It is also significant to note a final issue discussed by the judge. An important part of the relationship between two parties (church and clergyperson) is "the relationship the parties believe they are creating." The judge noted that receipt of a W-2 from the church "would mitigate against self-employment" while receipt of a 1099-MISC "would mitigate against the status as an employee."

What are the long-term implications of the Cosby case? First, it would substantiate the long-standing position that clergy have a unique relationship with the churches they serve more closely resembling an independent contractor than an employee. Next it suggests that clergy claiming self-employed status should insist upon a 1099-MISC from the congregation rather than a W-2 form.

The complete text of *Cosby v. Commissioner* is available from Clergy Financial Services, P.O. Box 6007, Grand Rapids, MI 49516. Send $1.00 and a self-addressed stamped envelope.

Concluding Unscientific Postscript

Well, pastor, you've come a long way. You've finished this book, but your journey of financial planning has only begun. Don't stop now.

You have a plan. Work your plan and your plan will work. Recognize that financial planning is a moving target. Strategies will need to be adapted as your goals change, if for no other reason because you have achieved your goals.

It's a satisfying feeling to know that you have achieved financial security. Your life will be more meaningful, your family will be in less jeopardy, and you will be free to become a more effective minister of Jesus Christ.

May God richly bless you and your journey.